I'm Able

a woman's advice for disability change agents

Sefakor G.M.A Komabu-Pomeyie, Ph.D.

Kate, thank you!

SGK

ONION RIVER

PRESS

Burlington, Vermont

Onion River Press
24 Maple Street, Suite 214
Burlington, VT 05401
www.onionriverpress.com

ISBN: 978-1-957184-31-9

Library of Congress Control Number: 2023909286

I dedicate this book to the Almighty God for keeping me safe and sound despite all the odds. My next dedication goes to my one and only son, Edonusem, who has been my strength. I cannot forget my late Mom and my late daughter Edomdedzi, who could not stay to see all my achievements and how I became "The Doctor Mama." I made it by God's grace. Finally, I dedicate this book to all my family and friends, people with disabilities globally, all advocates and everyone working with people with disabilities in the world.

Contents

Foreword

When I assumed the position as president of the non-profit World Learning and its Graduate School for International Training (SIT) in 2013, it seemed that everyone in the organization was talking about a recent Ghanaian master's recipient, Sefakor Komabu Pomeyie. "Our most dynamic and strategic advocate in decades," one long-time professor said. "A talented orator with a gift for energizing others," said another. The dean of students was more direct: "She's dynamite." Rarely in the flood of praise, by the way, did anyone mention that she had overcome the challenge of a severe disability.

True, Sefakor had been chosen by her classmates to be their commencement speaker; was soon to win the prestigious Advancing Leaders Fellowship Award and other honors; and was asked by the Board of Directors to give the keynote at a vital annual fundraising event in New York City. But could she really be that impressive? Privately, I worried about the Board's decision to put our financial well-being in the hands of a recently graduated foreign student.

My concerns vanished immediately after Sefakor took the stage in a Manhattan conference hall. Magically, the entire audience was transported to a small town in Ghana where an 8-year-old Sefakor contracted polio and was transformed from an active playful tot into one who struggled to even crawl. Her community shunned her, viewing her malady as a sign from the heavens of a curse on their town. One village elder urged Sefakor's mother to abandon her to die in the nearby forest. Even her own father forsook her and soon left Sefakor and her mother to fend for themselves.

Sefakor not only survived, but she also thrived. She drew on two powerful sources of strength: her faith in a merciful and benevolent God, and her mother's faith in her. Step by painful step, Sefakor used her disability not as a crutch but as a shield against the taunts and discrimination she faced. Over the years, with little or no accommodation, she excelled at high school, university, and teachers' college, racking up honor after honor. Speaking regularly on national media and at regional churches, she became, in her own words, "an unofficial voice and poster girl for disabilities."

Before long, she had earned a Ford Fellowship to obtain her master's degree at SIT in Brattleboro, Vermont. Sefakor finished her presentation that evening by reminding the audience that even in the United States, she faced alienation and prejudice due to her disability and her ethnicity. "The inclusion and accommodation required by Americans with Disabilities Act of 1990 is a promissory note that remained unpaid," she concluded.

As she ended, the audience stood in unison and showered her with thunderous applause and cheering. And incidentally, they opened not just their hearts but their wallets and purses to promote inclusion programs at World Learning.

In this moving and insightful book you are about to enjoy, Sefakor brings the story up to the present, describing both her personal tragedies and professional triumphs over the past decade. The triumphs include the founding of an international disability advocacy group called "Enlightening and Empowering People with Disabilities in Africa" (EEPD AFRICA) and her earning a doctorate from the University of Vermont during the COVID pandemic, gaining her the nickname, Doctor Mama. Even though she lost the mother and her own daughter, in this journey, she sill has reasons to be grateful to God and people around her.

To end on a personal note, Sefakor rightly states in her introduction, "Disability is an open-ended majority class that anyone can join at any point in time." My entry came in 2015, when I was diagnosed with Parkinson's Disease (PD), an incurable but rarely fatal neurological malady. In the process of my accepting and ultimately embracing my ailment, Sefakor's wise council, deep friendship and powerful example have helped show the way. I now appreciate that

PD has deepened my understanding of the challenges and discrimination facing others with more serious ailments and led me to a more relaxed "don't sweat the small stuff" mindset. Doctor Mama is my guide, my ally, and my hero. She is about to become yours as well.

Ambassador Donald Steinberg
Falls Church, Virginia
July 2, 2023

Introduction

Disability is an open-ended majority class that anyone can join at any point in time. This is because people with disabilities are the largest and most diverse minority within the population, representing all abilities, ages, races, ethnicity, religions, and socioeconomic backgrounds. Those who become people with disabilities, visible or invisible, by birth or after birth, do not go to the market to bargain for the type they want. Like it or not, destiny may find you in this club along your life journey. If this is the offer given in this life, you best own it.

In this personal life narrative, you will see how the author's mother accepted her daughter's disability and encouraged her to accept her condition and move forward. The acceptance level of every person with a disability is their armor and strength to face and break any systemic barrier in this unjust world. Failure to own one's disability makes the journey more difficult and gives way to acceptance of any garbage thrown on you by society.

This book opens the mind of every reader, whether you are a person with or without a disability, and prods you to come out of your comfort zone to analyze. You, as the reader, will think a bit deeper, because at the end of each chapter, you need to build on the author's experience, connect to the real world, and judge for yourself if people with disabilities deserve the exclusion, marginalization, and discrimination they go through systemically. You will be moved, at your own pace, to solve some systemic changes based on the fact that you would not like to associate yourself with the horrific practices the author herself was subjected to. At the end, you will embrace disability, acknowledge that it is a part of humanity, and we are all in it together.

Each chapter ends with two or more questions for the reader. One question invites personal introspection and the other encourages the system's change. Many chapters include opportunities to apply deeper analysis to social justice issues raised in the chapter.

By the end of the book, readers who have accepted the author's challenge in each chapter will be better connected to their community, taking action, and advocating in multiple small ways to make the change needed in their community.

Readers can also expect to make a new friend and mentor in Sefakor. Experiencing another's story allows us to see them, identify personally with shared challenges, and be inspired to follow their example. Readers will feel as if they are sitting beside the author as her story unfolds as an intimate first-person account. Readers also have the honor of sitting next to Sefakor's mother and grandmother, who both raised her on African wisdom and deep spirituality.

Chapter 1
The Comforter

"We will name her Sefakor—my God has comforted me—if we end up having a baby girl," said my joyful father. My mom, out of curiosity, asked him, "What if it's a boy?" My dad answered, "Dzidzornu. We'll name him Dzidzornu because indeed, he's a gift of happiness."

The meaning of the two names is the same in principle; happiness! Sefakor, because no matter where they find themselves in life, they believe God cares about them so much as to bring them a comforter to warm their hearts and spark happiness into their lives. Dzidzornu, because a child is a gift from God, and this gift isn't just a mere gift but rather a gift that brings rays of hope and happiness into the parents' daily lives.

Where I come from, names are not just names. In Ghana, names carry meaning and are usually given as a reflection of the kind of life the child is supposed to live. "Before I formed you in the womb, I knew you," says the Lord in Jeremiah 1:4-5. Before my eyes could witness the magnificence of this life, I had a name, and the name simply means "my Comforter—their comforter."

The world became my playground when I came in. I don't remember the days I was learning to crawl or the times I was learning to walk, but from the accounts of people who were around, I was energetic and bubbly. Then I learned to walk. They say I was born in November, 1975 and I was always running around and jumping over things my little legs could not fly me over. They wondered where my energy came from, and with my now-adult mind, I want to believe that energy came from the love and care I received from Mom and Dad every day. They were ever watchful over me, and that made me feel I could do anything without fear. When Mom's eye was over me, what could ever hurt me? When Dad is around screaming "stop" with his masculine voice, I was assured that he could scream my troubles away and I would be just fine. So I didn't have any fear and could afford to jump around, run around, and pretend I was flying.

One day, when I was six or seven, Dad returned from work. Immediately, he took off his uniform and went straight to the kitchen where Mom was cooking. I have no memory of what Mom was cooking, but I remember Dad was with her throughout. He picked up utensils and washed them. When Mom needed something, he ran and fetched it for her. They laughed about something I didn't know, and Dad snuck behind Mom and tickled her unexpectedly. Mom jerked from fear, but when she realized it was Dad, they both burst out laughing very loudly.

I was a child, yet to be taught about the roles of men and women when it comes to marriage, so I didn't get the significance of what the two were doing. What rather caught my attention was the smile on my father's face as he went about in the kitchen cooking with my mom. My mom laughed a lot, and it was obvious she enjoyed the tickles. The laughter between them was the secret that made me a happy child. When the home is happy, everything within it, including kids who barely know what love is, becomes happy.

The relationship between my mom and dad was different compared to that of the other couples who lived in the same vicinity. It was very difficult to see a man laundering clothes because it was a woman's job. But my dad wasn't like that. He'd sit next to Mom with the washing bowl in front of them. They would both wash together, all the while giggling and laughing about jokes only the two of them found funny. Mom rinsed the clothes while Dad picked them up and hung them on the drying line. They were like two peas in a pod, but not because they resembled each other. The two simply found comfort in each other's presence and loved to be in the same space with each other.

Dinner times were some of my favorite moments. It was the moment when the attention wasn't on the food cooked for the night but rather on me and ensuring I got fed to my satisfaction. Dad would lift me up and place me in the middle of the table on which the food was served. Dad would fetch some food with his hand and put it in my mouth. Mom wouldn't sit and watch so she'd join. She'd fetch and put in my mouth, and Dad would also fetch and put in my mouth. At some point, they would both have food in their hands, competing for my attention. "Let's see whose food she's going to take," Dad would say. They both held their hands up in my face and simultaneously shouted, "ahhhhm...ahhhhm."

It made me happy. It made me feel special and it brought a lot of happiness to my tiny heart.

My dad met Mom in the 1960s in Accra. He was a policeman working at the police depot as a quartermaster. My mom was a simple librarian working at Accra Girls Secondary School. From the police depot to Accra Girls is about a fourteen-minute drive. The traffic situation in Accra wasn't as dire in the 1960s as it is today, so I can imagine how easy it was for my dad to move from his working station to the school and my mom.

My mom didn't tell me about the beginning of their relationship, let alone exactly what my dad told her to make her fall in love with him. I won't blame her for not telling me. If I did ask her, knowing who my mother was, she would have given me all the details concerning their beginning. My uncle, my father's younger brother, was there right from the start. He was living with my father, in the same house, when my father fell in love with my mother. I can imagine my dad returning home in the evening and telling him the story of a wonderful woman he had met. I can imagine my dad describing my mom and telling him about his intention to make her his wife. When men fall in love, they talk to people close to them about it. I believe my dad did the same, so I reached out to my uncle to ask about the beginning of my parents.

He said, "The two of them were inseparable love birds. There was no him without her, and since they were not living far apart, he was always on his way to meet her." According to my uncle's account, my dad knew right from the beginning that my mom was the one for him, so he didn't waste much time before he proposed. I want to believe the ethnicity of my parents also played a key role in their love affair right from the beginning. Both Mom and Dad were of the Anlo (a south-eastern ethnic group) extraction.

My dad came from Tegbi, a small town closer to Keta in the Volta region. My mother came from Dzelukorfe and Whuti. Dzelukorfe is not far from Keta, and the town's claim to fame comes from the fact that the mother of Jerry Rawlings, Ghana's Former President (from 1981 – 2001), was born there. Tegbi and Dzelukorfe are not far from each other, so finding a woman in a new place who speaks your language and comes from a town close to your own gives you common fertile ground on which to build a relationship. And when that woman is as modest and well-groomed as my mother was, marriage wasn't a difficult decision to make.

After a few months of dating, my dad made the decision to marry my mother.

My dad didn't want the marriage ceremony to be an ordinary one, so he planned it to coincide with the Hogbetsotso festival. The Hogbetsotso festival is celebrated by the Anlo people. It's usually celebrated on the first Saturday of November, and during that period, Anlo people from all over the world travel home to witness the festival and celebrate the legendary exodus and heroism of the Ewe-Dogbo people from a tyrant king. It is a homecoming period, and my dad was sure all his family members and my mother's family members would be home during the festival. In his mind, "If I'm going to have a grand marriage ceremony, then it better be at a time when everyone is home to witness it."

A few months before November, my dad sent his people to my mother's home to perform the knocking ceremony and make my father's intention to marry my mother known. It was during the knocking ceremony that a date was fixed for the main marriage ceremony in November.

According to my uncle, the marriage ceremony was a spectacle to behold. My mom was decorated and presented to my dad in a blissful ceremony which became the talk of the town for a very long time. It was a moment where two people of the land had met outside of it and had come back home to seek blessings from their kindred. The love in their eyes that day was visible for all to see and the smiles from their lips confirmed the love they both proclaimed for each other.

With their fingers intertwined, they walked off the stage, and after a few days traveled back to Accra to begin life as husband and wife.

"Did it take so long after marriage before I was born?" I asked my uncle. He answered, "I can't clearly recall how long it took, but I can confidently say it took them less than a year to conceive you."

Less than a year later, my mom walked up to my dad and said, "I think I'm pregnant."

My dad had this grin on his face when he asked, "You think you're pregnant or you know you're pregnant?"

My mom had to see the doctor at Korle-Bu to have it confirmed that indeed, she was pregnant.

The kind of joy that enveloped my parents at the confirmation of the pregnancy can't be put into words. I wasn't there to witness it, but it always brings me ceaseless joy when I think of it. Knowing I was happy news to my parents makes me want to do more for people I encounter every day so they too can experience that joy I once brought to my parents.

In the mornings, Dad would put on his uniform, drive Mom to work, and send me to school. I wouldn't see him again until later in the evening. I didn't know where he went to and I didn't know this place called 'work' where my dad went every morning. Maybe I asked him about it and he said, "Wait. I will take you there one day," or I didn't, but one morning, Dad came for me at school. He sat me down in the police van and drove away. I thought we were going home. If we were, we would have gone to pick up Mom, but we didn't. He kept driving until we got to a place and he told me, "This is where I work. This is where I come to when I put on my uniform each morning." I turned my eyes and started looking around. It looked like a place I'd never seen before. There were so many other men and women dressed like my dad. "Let's go to my office," he said as he held my hand and pulled me along.

I saw a lot of faces I hadn't seen before. One of them, a man, asked my dad, "Is that your daughter?" Dad responded, "Yeah, she's my little angel." The man walked up to me, stooped, and touched my cheeks; "How are you, little girl?" I don't remember how I responded to him. I might have shrunk like little kids do when they meet new people. One of the officers gave me a toy to play with, which I later took home. It was aɲevidzi, a rubber doll that cries like a baby when pressed hard in the chest. I was so fascinated by that doll that I slept with it that night. I took it to school the next day. I took it to church the following Sunday. There was nowhere I didn't go without my aɲevidzi until one day, it went missing.

Sundays were another special day in the lives of my parents. They were both staunch Presbyterians and never missed a day in church. They took me along every Sunday. At first, we all worshipped in the main chapel, but according to my mom, they found it very hard to contain me. I couldn't sit still. I didn't know the difference between the church and the playing field, I didn't know what behavior was expected of me in the chapel, and I ran around when everyone was supposed to sit still in the presence of the Lord. I screamed at the top of my voice when congregants were supposed to remain quiet and pray silently. I was only a child whose main aim was to make play out of every situation.

That meant my parents had to interrupt their personal worship to keep an eye on me. When I ran, they ran after me. When I screamed, they covered my lips with their hands. So eventually, they took me to the Sunday school where kids like me belonged.

They didn't leave me there at the Sunday school. They sat with me and watched me play and learn to pray. They were with me when I learned my first song and learned how to dance. Every Sunday in church, my parents were with me at the Sunday school because they couldn't take their eyes off me. So, they were supervising me interchangeably.

The three of us formed a bond you could not put asunder—Mom, Dad, and me. It was always us together. I was a child. I didn't understand so many things in life. For instance, I didn't understand why it had to rain and didn't know where the sun came from. I didn't know why Mom went on her knees with her hands clasped in front of her and whispered to no one. My little brain didn't understand so many things, but this I understood very well; I understood my parents' love for me through the way they looked at me when I was just walking around being a child. I also understood that for me to remain happy, Dad and Mom had to always be present—to help me bathe, put on my clothes and send me to school. It took the two of them to achieve that all the time and I needed them to always be there to see me through.

But the tides changed, and the dynamic of the love between Mom and Dad shifted. I didn't know so much, but when the changes came, I felt them. I saw them through my mother's eyes, and I felt it through the many inactions of my father. It was like the rainbows of our lives were fading and none of us could do anything about it. When the fever started that night, I trusted my parents to make it all go away. But it was that fever that changed everything in my life and in the lives of my once-upon-a-time very loving parents.

CHAPTER ONE QUESTIONS:

–In Ewe culture, family does not only mean parents with their children. The traditional Ghanaian family patterns itself after the African model of patriarchy, or men holding power and controlling wealth and decisions.

–What does family mean to you?

–Who has power in your family?

–Where do you find your family root and how do you connect to this lineage? How has your own family structure/dynamic changed over time?

Chapter 2
The Fever

I was 8 years old. I had returned from school in the afternoon feeling very sick. My mom touched my forehead with the back of her hand and said, "You're running a very high temperature." She didn't think much out of my high temperature until I started feeling very weak and restless. That evening, she rushed me to the hospital. It wasn't the police hospital where we usually went for medical care. Dad was traveling and my mom reasoned it would be very difficult for us to access quick medical care at the police hospital without my dad present.

Mom carried me on her back to the nearest private hospital. My sickness was diagnosed as fever, so they gave me an injection and some drugs, and later that very day, I was discharged. The drugs should have made me feel better, but they didn't. I was so weak I couldn't stand on my feet or sit on my buttocks. I had to lie down all the time while Mom did everything for me.

Soon my dad returned from his travel and realized I wasn't feeling well. He asked what the issue was and Mom told him I'd been sick. He asked, "If she's sick why don't you take her to the hospital?" Mom answered, "I took her to the private hospital on the other side of town and they said she has a fever. They gave her injections and some drugs, but there hasn't been any improvement in her condition."

Dad's demeanor immediately switched from calm to furious. "Why not the police hospital instead of that private hospital?" he asked angrily. With calm in her voice, Mom explained, "Your daughter's situation was critical. We needed to see the doctor quickly and you were not here to aid us through that laborious bureaucracy at the police hospital, so I thought it wise to go to that private hospital where she could see a doctor immediately."

Dad's anger wasn't necessarily about the hospital Mom decided to take me to. His anger was financially charged. At the police hospital, he wouldn't have paid any medical bills, but my mom took me to a place that made a dent in his pocket. From there, the argument shifted from my health to whether or not my mom made a good decision. Dad spoke angrily to my mom, questioning the rationale of her choice. My mom was resolute. She argued, "Given the circumstances I found myself in, I made a good decision. That private hospital has a good stock of drugs compared to the police hospital where they write the prescription for you to buy at the counter. My daughter's life first before anything."

For a couple of minutes, they stood face to face exchanging words. That was the first time I ever saw my mom and dad fiercely arguing. Dad walked to my bed, touched my forehead with the back of his hand, and said, "I hope she gets better." Then he walked away.

Hope has a way of disappointing you when hope is all you have. I didn't get better. I got worse. Day by day my situation spiraled toward doom. I was so weak and couldn't move my lower limbs. I was sent back to the hospital, where the doctors examined me. One of the doctors used a needle to pinch my right leg. After each pinch, he'd ask, "Do you feel anything?"

I answered, "Yeah, I can feel the sharp piercing of the needle."

He did the same test on my left leg and unfortunately, I couldn't feel anything. He kept asking me, "Don't you feel the piercing of the needle?" I shook my head. The doctor turned to my mother and said, "Your daughter has paralytic polio. She's gradually losing her reflexes and she won't be able to walk again."

I didn't understand much of what the doctor said, but the look on my mother's face said it all. *Whatever I'm suffering from might be grievous*, I thought. When Mom started crying, she confirmed the fears in my mind. I asked her, "Mom, am I going to die?"

She responded firmly while wiping the tears off her face. "No, you're not going to die. We serve a living God."

According to the World Health Organization, poliomyelitis (polio) is a highly infectious viral disease that largely affects children under 5 years of age. The virus is transmitted person-to-person, or less frequently, by contaminated water or food.

The virus multiplies in the intestine and from there invades the nervous system and causes paralysis.

Polio has no cure, but it is vaccine-preventable. In the 1980s, information on polio was very scant, especially among the rural dwellers of Ghana. Because of how devastating the disease is, most rural dwellers believed it was a curse or a punishment from the gods. My mother was educated and knew about polio. I was born in one of the biggest hospitals in Ghana where they had access to polio vaccines.

According to my mom, I got the vaccination five days after I was born, but something went wrong. The vaccine I received had expired. During Acheampong's (a former military ruler of the Republic of Ghana) regime, many consumer goods were hoarded, creating artificial shortages so merchants of such goods could make excessive profits. Unfortunately, the polio vaccines the government received at that time had been hoarded. These drugs spent many years in a warehouse and had expired by the time they were released to the hospitals.

I happened to be one of the unfortunate babies who received the expired vaccine. I was empty when I got infected with polio. I was like a house without defense, and like a knife through butter, polio exerted its devastating effects on me. I was physically broken for so many months. I was bedridden. I couldn't walk or sit. I was so weak, it felt like my own body was fighting against me.

I had been a bubbly child who loved to run and jump around. I could stand on one leg and whirl around for several minutes until I had a bout of vertigo. I would laugh and scream about the feeling and shout to my friends, "Hey see, it looks like the world is spinning—everything around me is moving." Polio took all that away and left me a weakling who could only crawl on her belly. That's not the only thing polio took from me. It also took away the joy in my family. Each morning, I lifted up my eyes to look at my mom's face, and all I saw was a cocktail of fatigue, hurt, depression, and sorrow. She hardly wore the beautiful smile she was known for. Her pain wasn't only for the child who was losing her mobility to polio. It was also about a love story that was gradually fading into nothingness.

Dad was drifting away. Since the day they had the argument about which hospital I should have been taken to, things never returned to normal. Dad refused to pay my hospital bills because I was taken to the hospital he did not sanction. Mom had to pay for it all. Dad stopped helping mom in taking care of me. Mom had to do everything. My situation embarrassed my dad, so he kept his distance. Having a daughter who crawls on her belly wasn't something he signed up for when he said he wanted a child. I remember one day I was lying on a mat at the center of our sitting room when we heard a knock on our door. It was visitors for my dad. He looked at my mom and told her, "Move that thing from there to the bedroom. I have visitors."

Mom got up, picked me up with the mat, and walked into the bedroom. When she laid me down, she sat at the edge of the bed and began crying. She didn't want me to see it. She turned her face away from me to hide the hurt. I saw it anyway. She was deeply hurt and it showed all over her body.

The news of my sickness spread around the vicinity, and it became a topic of gossip. Some said it was a curse and others believed the gods were punishing us for the mistakes of our forefathers. Some came to see me with pity in their eyes and others came with sympathy. One quiet dawn, we heard a knock on our door. Nobody responded the first time because it was unusual for someone to knock on a neighbor's door at that ungodly hour. Seconds later, the person knocked again. Mom asked, "Who is it?"

The voice responded, "It's me, open up. I'm here to help."

The voice sounded familiar. It was the voice of an old woman who lived in the neighborhood. *At this time?* Mom might have thought, but she slowly walked over to the door and opened it up. Right at the door, she asked the woman, "Please, what brought you here so early this dawn?"

The woman responded, "I've seen your daughter's condition and I see how you're suffering day in and day out trying to help her. Her condition isn't medical. It is spiritual. It is a curse from the gods and it's not going to go away anytime soon, but you know how people of her kind are treated. They don't deserve to live among us, so if you're ready, I'll help you to throw her into the evil forest in our village."

Mom was startled. She was so angry, she didn't know what to tell this old woman. She pointed away and screamed at her, "Leave my house... leave my house and never step a foot here!"

She didn't even stand there to watch the woman leave. She slammed the door and walked back into the room, still angry and talking to herself.

Mom may have been dialoguing with herself to calm her own rattled spirit, for she had grown up knowing the fate of "spirit children." For generations, beliefs have persisted that children who are sick or have disabling conditions are out of favor with God. Elders prescribe poison drinks or advise parents to abandon or bury their "spirit children" outside of villages. This ancient practice, also perpetrated in neighboring countries, would become illegal in Ghana, but not until 2013.

Dad refused to help and continued keeping his distance from me. He walked around the house wearing a ceaseless frown. He changed completely. He stopped going to church. Maybe at the corner of his heart, he felt God had disappointed him. He barely stayed in the house and mostly returned home in a drunken stupor. He wouldn't look at me and wouldn't allow strangers to see who I had become. The house was always tense whenever he was around—no more laughter and no more walking to the kitchen to tickle my mom. It looked like my condition had sucked up the joy and playfulness that once upon a time filled our home. Before my polio, Dad and Mom never quarreled or fought. After polio, they were almost always fighting about one thing or another.

I was still lying on my belly, unable to sit or crawl. I was suffering and my dad's attitude towards us did nothing to help. He preferred keeping me in the dark to bringing me into the light where everyone will see me and cause him shame. I was always in the room, learning to crawl on my belly and learning to feed myself. On Sundays, Mom strapped me on her back and took me to church. In church, I learned a lot of Christian songs and sang them for comfort when I was alone. On weekdays, Mom again strapped me on her back and took me to her place of work, Accra Girl's Library. At the library, Mom placed me under her table while she went about doing her work. She occasionally brought me some books to flip through, and I looked at pictures while Mom was busily working.

For close to a year, I remained on the ground and made little movement crawling on my belly. Mom came home one day saying someone had shown her a place where they could help me walk again. The next day, Mom strapped me on her back again and took me to there: Accra Limb Fitting Center, which was located at the Tema Lorry Station in Accra. They did some checks on me and took me through a series of physical therapy. I was scheduled to visit the facility on weekends to continue with the therapy. Each weekend, Mom strapped me behind her back and took me to the Limb Fitting Center.

I started seeing improvement in my body, but the relationship between Mom and Dad kept deteriorating. Dad had completely stopped being a dad to me and had completely stopped being the husband he used to be to my mother. It was like a battleground where my mother and I belonged to one side and my dad to the other. On my father's side, I was an embarrassment he had to avoid by all means. It wasn't my fault that things turned out the way they did. It wasn't my mom's fault that a fever took away my limbs, but Dad wouldn't see it that way. One morning, we woke up to find a letter in the center of the table. It was Mom who picked up the letter. She noticed the handwriting and immediately knew it was my dad who had written it.

I remember Mom silently reading the letter to herself. She looked heavenward and started reading aloud. I was only nine years old, and I don't remember what was written in the letter word for word, but I remember he mentioned the shame I'd brought to him and his extended family. How I'd reduced him from a respectable police officer to a man who has a crippled daughter. He talked about hardship and talked about being tired of everything. There was one line in the letter that never left my memory—the point where my dad referred to me again as "That Thing." He wrote, "I cannot live with That Thing anymore."

I sobbed over it and felt guilty for being the reason my dad had to leave. Being crippled was enough of a burden on my young soul, but being referred to as a "thing" by the person who owes me all the love and care in this world, paralyzed my heart with worthlessness. After so many years, I still remember that line. I hold no grudges, but somehow, that line was carved into a part of me that would be very difficult to erase.

After reading the letter, Mom opened the window and looked outside as if to catch a last glimpse of him before he disappeared, but he was nowhere to be found. He was already gone. He walked out of our lives and never did he look back—not even once.

CHAPTER 2 QUESTIONS:

- What influence has cultural beliefs about disability had on you and your family?

- How do these beliefs impact disability law and social policy across your country and around the world?

- Do you believe that disability is part of humanity or not? What influences your answer?

- How do cultural beliefs about disability show up in first-person narratives, the media, art and literature, academia, and professional discourse and practice?

Chapter 3
The Miracle

Oh, how I wish I could mention Mom's name to you throughout the book, but culturally, that is a sign of disrespect to our elders. We never called our parents or elders by their first names as Americans do. All the same, I would like you to know my mom's name. I called her Mom, but her maiden name is Josephine Yawo Kudowor. Mom had always been alone in the journey of seeking good health for me. Dad didn't help with anything. Though he was physically around, he was emotionally absent, so Mom had to do everything by herself. Since he was there with us, people might have been under the erroneous impression that he was helping to take care of me or supporting us in some way. When he left, his absence became obvious, so people, including my grandma, might have formed the impression that Mom would begin to suffer the burden alone. That might have compelled my grandma, Mamaga, to ask my mom to send me over to her in Anloga. Mamaga wanted to take care of me so Mom could have a sound mind to concentrate on her job.

Mom gave the request some thought but in a different way. Yes, she needed a hand in taking care of me, but she didn't think sending me away was a good idea. She loved me too much to do without me, so she decided to move back home to Anloga where she'd be closer to her own mother who was living in Whuti. She put in an application for transfer from Accra Girls' Secondary School to Zion College in Anloga District, which was later granted. So, in the later years of the 1980s,

Mom packed our bags, and baggage, and left for Anloga, leaving behind all the memories of a once-upon-a-time beautiful marriage that ended with just a letter.

I don't remember our first day in Anloga, but I can imagine Grandma welcoming us with open arms and a smiling face. I can imagine her saying to Mom, "Vinye, woezor." I can also imagine the smile on my mother's face when she responded, "Akpe." Finally, we were at a place where we could speak our native language to everyone we met on the road and not some selected few. This is home—where the tongue speaks freely in the language of our birth.

It's usually very hard to make new beginnings, but my grandma was there right from the start to make things easier for us. In the mornings before she went to work, Mom would send me to my grandma's place in Whuti. Somedays she'd come back for me and some days she wouldn't, but either way, I was in safe hands. I loved the way my grandma spoke to me; she always had words of motivation and stories that lifted my dull spirit.

My grandma believed in the healing hands of God, too. In her own words, "Medicine alone can't heal broken bones and make the paralyzed soul walk. It's when we invite God into our medications that medicines are able to realize their full healing potential. You know by his wounds you have been healed," she quoted from the book of Peter 2:24. Behind Grandma's house was a Pentecostal church. It wasn't far from where we lived—just two blocks away. Each morning, Grandma carried me on her back to the church premises. She was old and weak, but when it came to church, she would gather the last juice of strength left in her and take me there.

From morning to evening, we would pray, share the word of God, sing praises and worship God, and pray again before we finally left for our individual homes. This continued every day from morning until evening. At some point, the church became my third home because I was always there, praying for a miracle. One morning, Grandma wasn't feeling too well. She looked at me and said, "I'm not in the best of shape today, but we still have to go to church." I asked her, "How do we get there, then? I can't walk, and you can't carry me because you're sick, so how do we go?" She responded, "There's always a way. You watch me."

The thought of not going to church saddened my heart so much. It had become a place for my healing, a place I met people who cared enough to help me reach God with my healing supplications. Apart from that, a girl who lacks mobility has very little to fill the hours of her days. If I didn't go to church and fill the hours with singing and prayers, what else could I do? The more I thought of not going to church that day, the sadder I became, and I felt rejected.

Not too long after Grandma had left, I heard the voices of people from behind our house. Soon, they were in front of the house. They said, "Grandma sent us to fetch you for church, so let's get going." One of them carefully picked me up and strapped me behind him, and took me to the church premises. You can imagine my happiness that day. From that day onward, it became the norm that if Grandma was too tired to carry me, she'd send some members of the church.

Mom wasn't left out of the church activities. Mostly, she would join us at church after school and stay with us until it was over so she could take me home. On weekends, Mom would guide me through the physical therapy training I was taught at the hospital to strengthen my limbs and waist. I never missed any of my medications. Morning, afternoon, and evening, Mom ensured that I took all of my drugs and went through the physical therapy exercises before I finally went to bed.

All the while, I hadn't been able to sit on my own or stand. It had been two years already and my legs had lost their use and became vegetated. I was always lying down, either on my back or prostrate. One afternoon, something great happened in my body. I remember it very clearly as though it happened to me only yesterday.

It was a Saturday morning, and as usual, I was at the church camp with Mom and Grandma. I remember lying on the floor surrounded by the church members. I couldn't lift my head to look at the faces of those surrounding me and praying for me. I was lying on my belly, so all I could see were their feet as they stamped on the ground and screamed out their prayers to the Lord. I laid there and prayed along. All of the sudden, I felt this sensation in my waist, and a slight tremor followed shortly. I laid still and silent, listening to what was going through my body. The group kept praying, clapping, and singing. The tremor happened again and this time it felt like something had shifted in my body. Then I felt this urge to get up from the floor. I hesitated because I hadn't sat for more than two years. But the urge got stronger until it sounded like a voice in my head; "Girl, get up from the floor and sit up. Just trust and obey, you'll be fine."

I started pulling myself together and the next thing I knew, I was sitting comfortably on the floor. Those in prayer opened their eyes to find me seated on the floor. They couldn't hold it together; they jumped up and screamed, "Praise the Lord, Hallelujah!" The drummers began playing their drums and the whole group burst into loud singing. Everyone present was so happy to see me sitting on the floor, my grandma especially. She didn't know what to say or do. She looked at me and said, "I knew this day would come. I knew you would one day get off the ground by the grace of God. What a great testimony. Thank you, God."

I couldn't believe what was happening to me, but I knew God is capable of this and more, so I sat there and clapped my hands as the drummers played and the singers sang.

From that day on, I didn't look back. I did all I could not to remain on the ground forever. I continued taking my drugs religiously. Physical therapy also continued. Every weekend, Mom helped me through the physical exercises that sought to strengthen my legs and my muscles. Not too long afterward, I started learning to crawl. I rested my weight on my two hands and knees and moved one arm and the opposite leg forward at the same time. When I wanted to stand, I did it with the aid of furniture or a wall. I was off the ground and that made me very happy. I didn't want to sit still. At every given opportunity, I crawled forward or tried to stand using furniture. I started helping with the house chores, especially the things I could do while seated on the floor.

I cleaned dishes and swept the floor with the broom. I could fold my mother's clothes and put them neatly in her wardrobe. If something could be brought down and fixed, I would gladly bring it down and fix it. Seeing the new energy and exuberance in me, Mom decided to carry me along whenever she was going to work. She no longer sent me to my grandma. Just like she did when we were in Accra, Mom put me under her desk in the library and brought me books to flip through. That was where I started learning the letters of the alphabet and numbers. It was under my mother's desk where I started learning how to count from one to ten.

◊

At some point, Mom decided I needed to go back to school. I had regained some sort of mobility and could crawl around. I was no longer sick and I could sit up and complete chores. Finding a school for me wasn't easy. Most schools were in the middle of the term and were no longer admitting pupils. They could only admit at the beginning of the following term. Mom continued bringing me to work and keeping me underneath her desk. Instead of flipping through just any book, she made a point to teach me the class one to class two curriculum so I wouldn't be behind when school started admitting pupils.

Eventually, I got admitted into Anloga RC School—the RC is an acronym for Roman Catholic. I yearned for school, but my first day in that school was an experience I would never forget. Mom took me to school that day wearing my new school uniform. I was happy when I was getting ready for school, but when I reached the school compound, my mood immediately changed. The happiness I felt when at home suddenly disappeared, and in its place was this unknown fear and loneliness. I don't know what changed or what I saw that robbed me of my excitement. It could have been the fact that for the first time in a long while, I was going to begin a new life in a new place where Mom wouldn't be around. She had always been my pillar. Being in school from morning until afternoon without my pillar scared me.

I looked around and all I saw were happy faces of kids walking around in pairs and holding hands as they moved into their various classes. I didn't see a crawling kid and that broke my heart. They all could walk, jump, and spin around if they needed to, but I was left on the ground crawling on both hands and knees. Suddenly, I didn't want my mom to leave me alone. I wanted to return home with her, but she looked into my eyes and said, "Ao my dear Fakor, you too belong here and if you're going to have a great future ahead of you, it starts from here. Go there and blend; you'll be all right."

I remember crying uncontrollably when Mom left me in the hands of my class teacher and began walking away.

The class was already arranged, and every kid had their seating position already, so I was asked to sit at the back of the class. All the kids in class turned and looked at me from time to time. I didn't know what they thought of me whenever they looked at me but I can imagine them asking themselves, "Why doesn't this one walk but crawl instead?" They found me strange and unwelcoming, so they all avoided me that day. That deepened my sense of loneliness, and I couldn't wait to go home to my mom.

Nothing changed the next day. Again, I cried when Mom left me there. The kids stood in groups and watched me as I crawled around. Nobody wanted to be my friend. I started finding excitement during lesson time. Our class teacher (I remember her name very well after all these years), Ms. Adjinku, asked a question in class, and no one could answer. I knew the answer, but I felt very timid to raise my hand and talk, so I sat quietly in my chair. After no one could answer the question, our teacher turned to me, "Yesss Sefakor, can you try to give us the answer?" I raised my head up and shyly gave out the correct answer. The whole class began clapping and shouting my name. I was so happy for myself, and for the first time in a long while, I felt some sense of accomplishment and belonging.

Things started changing around the class from that day on. During break time, one of the kids walked up to me. Her name was Mawukoenya. She said, "Hey, it's break time. Let's go for a break together." I got up from my chair and crawled by her side as we both went to where we could get food to buy. She had me sit under a tree close by and ran to get food for both of us. She became my friend in the class and we were seen together most times. But that friendship didn't last as long as I wanted it to. One morning, I went to school and didn't see Mawukoenya. I got worried. Without her, I was back to being lonely. I went to the teacher and asked the whereabouts of my friend. She answered, "Oh your friend is not coming back to school again. She left the town with her parents, and they'll find a new school for her where they went to settle." That broke my heart because, without her, I was going to be lonely, and indeed I went through the rest of the term without any friends. I did not have any friend who would hold my school uniform up for me to prevent it from soaking into people's pee in the bathroom. Since then, anytime I went to pee, my body will be smelling of pee from the bathroom because my uniform would be soaked.

One sunny afternoon, after break time, our class teacher said we were going to do mental and dictation. Mental was something I dreaded. The teacher gave you a math problem and allotted just a few seconds for you to figure out the answer. I wasn't good at mathematics, and the speed with which you were required to answer the mental questions was too fast for me to come to terms with. I loved dictation because I knew how to spell a lot of words. While under my mom's table at the library, she taught me how to pronounce certain words and how one could easily spell those words, so I was very comfortable with dictation.

That afternoon, our class teacher took her time to pronounce the English words one after the other and asked us to write the spelling in our books. Five words, I remember. After the exercise, she took our books to mark our work. After marking, it turned out that I was the only one who got all the spellings correct. I was so elated that I didn't know what to do with myself. Though I scored zero in the mental exercise, the English spelling test made up for it. I remember the looks on the faces of my classmates when the teacher announced to them that I was the only one who got all the spelling correct. They were amazed. They all turned to look at me. The teacher said, "There was this word I thought all of you would get wrong due to how complicated the spelling is, but Sefakor managed to get that one correct also. That's splendid—clap for her!" The whole class clapped, and it made my heart soar with pride. The word the teacher was talking about: margarine.

After this feat, I remember a lot of my classmates started warming up to me. They would come to me with their books and ask me to teach them how to spell certain words. They wanted to score a perfect mark in the next spelling test, so they came to me one after the other and it was at that point I started making friends again. People will come to you when you have something to give. I learned this lesson that day. In the eyes of my classmates, I was different; I didn't walk like them. Maybe they didn't come close to me because they didn't know how to relate to a girl who doesn't walk but instead crawls. But that day, when they realized there was something they could take from me, my inability to walk didn't matter. What mattered was what they could benefit from me. I didn't care about the fact that they were not friends with me. I was there and I could help, so I did help without thinking about how they treated me before that day.

CHAPTER 3 QUESTIONS:

－Most Africans are very religious and spiritual. There is an African proverb that says, "No matter how beautiful and well-crafted a coffin might look, it will not make anyone wish for death."

How do you explain this proverb in terms of disability and spiritual beliefs?

－Do you have belief systems or practices in your culture? Do these beliefs and practices free the people with disabilities in your community or do they put them in bondage?

Chapter 4
The Mirror

In 1984, Mom got a promotion. She became the Chief Librarian, and as a result, was transferred to Agbozume Secondary School, now called Somè Senior High School. That meant I had to say goodbye to my classmates and teachers in Anloga RC and follow Mom to Agbozume. A new place, a new beginning. I had to start a new school, find new friends, and begin life anew. Starting school life in Anloga RC had been very difficult. Starting school at National in Agbozume was not any less difficult. I started in class four and I went through the hardship all over again. It was as if my life had been reversed and I had to go through all the pains again: the rejection, the mockery, and the heartbreaks. All the pains I thought I had left behind kept replaying right in front of my eyes. The only difference was how I responded to them.

No one goes through the furnace of life and returns as the same person. Something changes and you feel it. You become a new person—either stronger than before or weaker. Life in Anloga RC had made me stronger and created in me a survivor's instinct. The taunting no longer bothered me. I'd been there before. The rejection didn't hurt any longer because I was there once. I walked in the face of humiliation with my head lifted up because I'd gone through worse. The Sefakor who cried when her mom left her in school was long dead and in her place was a new Sefakor who didn't care about the opinions of others. I was called "stubborn" because I didn't bend to their will. This new me might have been boosted by the fact that I was no longer crawling. I was walking with assistance. When we got to Agbozume, Mom was able to secure calipers and crutches for me so I could stand and walk.

It got to a point where the taunting and name-calling became too much. I felt that if I allowed them to continue without a fight, they were not going to stop, so I started picking fights with mates who never stopped teasing me. I remember the fight between me and Michael very well. He was taller than me so he thought he could bully me easily. He called me crooked and pointed at my legs and laughed at me. I told him, "Stop it, Michael, before I hurt you." He laughed hysterically and asked, "What can you do to hurt me, Madam Cripple?"

The mention of cripple got me so infuriated that I picked up a stone and threw it at him. He was so confident I was going to miss, but unfortunately for him, the stone landed heavily on his forehead and gave him a cut. He placed his palm on his forehead in an attempt to stop it from bleeding. A few seconds later, blood began dripping off his hands. That got me a little bit scared. I screamed, "I told you to stop but you wouldn't. You see what you've made me do to you?"

That evening, I was home with my mom when we heard a knock on our door. Mom opened it and it was Michael and his mother. His mother was livid. She told my mom, "See what your daughter did to my son in school today? I don't like any trouble between us, but I'm taking my son to the hospital and you're going to pay the bills." The next day, Michael came to school with plaster covering his forehead. He didn't stop taunting me. He didn't want to accept the fact that I'd defeated him, so I threw up a challenge to him; "If you think you're a man enough, meet me behind the classroom block after school and let's fight. Behind the classroom block was well known to be the zone for fighting. I would go there to watch fights or to fight people. While on the ground, I would ask them to come closer so that I beat them. In our language, they named the place Teva. I told him to meet me there. He kept running his mouth, but when the school closed, he was nowhere to be found. He later told me, "It's not that I can't fight you. My mom advised me to stay away from you because you're evil."

Indeed, he listened to his mother's advice and left me alone. That incident sent a strong message to my mates: that I wasn't a weakling after all and no one could walk over me easily just because of my condition.

Later that year, I joined the drama group of my school, National. They thought I couldn't act. They brushed me aside even before I was given the chance to prove what I could do. I kept pushing for a role until one day they gave me a chance. It was a play about the slave trade. The teacher told me, "You're going to play William Wilberforce, a British politician who fought for the abolition of the slave trade in the 1780s." It didn't matter that I was a girl asked to play a man. I acted the role with passion and delivered my lines with the eloquence of a girl who knew what was at stake. I felt that it was one chance for me to prove what I could do, and I didn't want to waste it.

All the teaching staff of the school and my schoolmates stood in awe as they watched me act with all the passion in me. I delivered my lines faultlessly. In the end, they all clapped and hailed me for how well I delivered. From then on, I became a prominent figure in the drama group. Most of the props we used while acting didn't favor my disability, so sometimes I fell and sustained bruises. That didn't stop me. Anytime I fell, I got up, dusted myself, and carried on. For the next two years in National Primary School, I acted with all diligence and tried as hard as I could to nail every role given to me. In class six, our drama group was selected to represent the local schools in the annual Sometutuza, a harvest festival of the people of Agbozume when chiefs and peoples of the region pay homage to and renew their allegiance to the paramount chief. Sometutuza usually follows within a few weeks' time of the Hogbetsotso festival of my parent's people.

That was like being invited to a feast with the king. It was a very huge occasion for the school and a proud moment for everyone in the drama group. For the next several weeks before the occasion, we rehearsed every day, making sure nothing would go wrong on the D-day. The night before the occasion, I remember lying in bed, looking at the ceiling, and playing my role in my imagination. I couldn't wait for daybreak to get up from bed, dress up, and show the world what I was capable of. The night was long but eventually, the cock crowed to usher in a new day—a day to be in the spotlight and show the world my acting skills.

I have very little memory of how the play went but I remember that after the performance, all the prominent people walked up to the stage to shake the hands of the performers. I shook the hands of the chiefs, great pastors, community leaders, and all the heads of school. Most of them hugged me and said a lot of kind words to me. My confidence soared, and at that moment I believed I could do anything regardless of my condition. I only had to believe in myself, practice my lines, and get up and dust myself whenever I fall. Indeed, I can do all things through Christ who strengthens me (Philippians 4:13).

◊

The following year I had to leave National Primary School. I had to leave because the school didn't have a junior secondary school. Kids who completed primary school there had to look for a different school that had a junior secondary level to attend. I gained admission into Kpota Junior Secondary School, also in Agbozume.

On the day before starting junior secondary school, my mom called me into the room and said, "Sit down, let me have a word with you." The look on her face when she said that was that of seriousness. She wasn't smiling. It felt like something serious had happened and she wanted me to know. I sat down in the chair in front of her thinking to myself, *I hope there's no problem.*

She began, "You're an adolescent now and now it's the time to know who you truly are so you can live life in a way that manifests the creator's intention for you. You haven't made it this far by sheer coincidence. It's been God since day one and I know He will continue to guide your steps for the rest of the journey ahead, but you have to do your part."

I sat there quietly with my right arm supporting my chin, listening to what she had to say. I was only a girl, twelve or thirteen years old. A few years prior, I was crawling on my belly with no future ahead of me. Families wrote me off and my father walked away thinking I was a useless case. The only one whose hands kept guiding me and whose words filled my soul with confidence in myself was my mom. She was the one who believed that I wasn't done yet, so she kept hope in me. So, if there was anyone I listen to and believe in her words, it was none other than my mom. That was why, that day, I sat quietly before her feet and listened carefully to what she had to say.

She continued: "If you had a reason to play while you were in primary school, this is the time to be serious. This is the time to take your books seriously. It's a very competitive world out there. You can't walk, so the world will always walk and leave you behind. The only thing that can push you in front of this world that's always running is education. That's why you don't have to joke with your books. As you move out there tomorrow, remember that the only friend you have is Jesus and the only tool you can rely on are your books."

She pointed at the mirror behind me and said, "Turn around and pick up the mirror for me." I clumsily got up from the chair, stretched my arms, and picked up the mirror. When I handed the mirror over to her, she asked, "If you look through the mirror, what do you see?" I answered, "Of course I see myself." She said, "Yes, you see yourself, but that's not the whole story. Look at yourself very well. Your upper body is very beautiful but you're crooked at the lower part of your body, so you need something to compensate for that. If you want to reach up and touch the world, you'll need a special support, and that support is your education. That's why you don't have to joke with it. The truth is, you can only walk but you can never run again. It is a miracle that you are walking and that is how God wants His image in you to be seen. Your running leg is education.

"No man will marry you for you to become a burden on him. You need to carry yourself first and add value to yourself before someone can be drawn to you. And you can only add value to yourself through education. Education will make you self-sufficient and independent. It's through education that you will realize your God-given potential and rub shoulders with the giants of this world. I will help you. I will do all I can to support you and give you the best so you can become who God wants you to become. You are my heroine, my precious stone, and my angel. You're my Kporkpormatsikoe and I know you will be great one day to the glory of God."

I was young, but what Mom told me that day thawed my adolescent spirit. I thought about it all day and went to bed thinking about it. When I woke up in the morning and dressed up for school, I knew what was expected of me and I knew what I had to give in order to achieve that. She did not stop prophesying in my life every day. She made sure I repeated positive words after her every morning before I left for school and evening before I went to bed. That was different from our regular prayers in doing this, we used the mirror!

For all three years I spent in Kpota Junior SS, I never took my books for granted. I didn't care about who liked me or who did not. I wasn't interested in the gossip whirling around about me and my disabilities. All I knew were my books and how to make the best use of them. Mom didn't stop reminding me about my goals in life. She never stopped talking about the mirror and the story of what I see when I look through it. She made a point to talk about it every morning after our devotion and all through school, and that advice became the signpost that guided me to the spot of my dreams.

At the end of junior secondary school, we sat for the Basic Education Certificate Examination. We were examined on twelve subjects, and when the results came out, I had made almost perfect grades. I have gotten ten one grades. The only person who did better than me was a boy who made eleven ones. I became the only female among four boys who qualified to go to senior secondary school.

CHAPTER 4 QUESTIONS:

–"What I am looking for is not out there, it is in me." —Hellen Keller, a prolific American author, lecturer, and disability advocate.

–What does my mother's mirror story mean to you?

–Disability is anybody's lot anytime. Do you see yourself in a similar mirror or not? Why?

–Have you had a similar mirror in life? How do you relate to other people's mirrors held up to your life?

Chapter 5
First Choice

The kind of grade I made in junior high school was one that gained a person admission into their first-choice school, but one couldn't be so sure since admission into schools was very competitive in the late 1980s in Ghana. You could make all the good grades and still miss the opportunity of attending an elite school of your choice. My first-choice school was Keta Secondary School, Ketasco. Growing up, all the best students in my community went to Ketasco. In the Volta Region where I came from, attending this school came with some sort of prestige you'd never find in attending any other school. It gave you respect among your equals and wrapped an aura of confidence around you wherever you went.

I knew I belonged there. I had worked hard enough to deserve it. In my mind, if I had admission into Ketasco, then everyone in the community would learn to respect my name because I had achieved something most daughters and sons in the community might not be able to achieve. They would finally realize that regardless of my condition, I still could make magic happen in my life.

I waited for the admission letter from Ketasco with careful optimism. One day I would say to myself, "They will pick me. I made good grades, so they definitely have to pick me." Another day, my faithless mind would kick in and say, "No they won't pick you. There are way too many people who made better grades and deserve it more than you do."

All I did was wait until one morning a letter came through for me; it was the admission letter from Ketasco. I screamed, "I knew it! I knew it was going to come eventually!" I started screaming out of joy. I thought I had a bigger heart but the joy that day couldn't find enough space in my heart to exist. My mom was there. She, too, was full of joy. She said a lot of things I don't remember now but the look on her face was that of a proud mom. I can imagine her telling herself, *Thank God for this favor you've done me and my daughter. As you said in your word, horses and chariots are prepared for battle, but victory comes from only you the Almighty. Thanks for giving us this victory. The child everyone brushed aside as a nonentity is now going to walk the corridors of a school most great people once walked.* It was in her behavior to first give thanks to God in everything.

When the dust of our joys settled, the problems of our lives started becoming clearer to us. It was like the story of the blind woman who was so excited about a gift a stranger gave to her as she sat by the roadside begging for food. It was only when she got home and opened the gift that she realized the gift that had made her so happy was actually a mirror. What use is a mirror to the blind? Like the blind woman, my admission brought a lot of joy to me and my mother, but later in the night, the obstacles between us and Ketasco started showing in our minds like a movie. All of these obstacles were enough for us to kiss the hope of going to my first-choice school goodbye.

Who was going to take care of me while at the boarding school? All my life, I strived to act and behave like an ordinary kid so I automatically invited other people to see me as an ordinary kid but no matter how you look at it, a kid like me had needs—"special needs." Ketasco didn't have the facilities to aid the movement of people with disabilities. Like most Ghanaian schools, this school was not accessible to people with mobility challenges.

As usual, the implementation of the inclusive education policy is still hanging on and nothing is happening practically. Policies are never coordinated with practices on the ground in the Ghanaian educational system. People with disabilities are still consciously and unconsciously discriminated against and excluded. There was no accommodation in place because it was not designed with people with disabilities in mind.

If I was going to survive at Ketasco, I needed someone to lean on emotionally, spiritually, and physically. I needed a mother, a friend, a sister, who'd be there for me—help me with my schoolwork, my home therapy, and personal care. I needed someone to help me walk around and be part of the school community. Someone to help me go through everyday life activities. Who was going to do that? Who was going to play the role of my mother in the boarding school?

Also, Mom didn't have the money to support me there. When she received my prospectus from the school, she went through all the items I was required to bring to school one after the other. She later looked up into the sky and shook her head. I can imagine her saying, "Where am I going to come up with this amount within this short period?" She had been alone in this battle of taking care of me for so long. Her finances were stretched, and she had gotten to a point where we were living from hand to mouth. It would have been easier for the camel to go through the eye of the needle than for my mom to raise that huge amount to send me to this boarding school.

The next morning, she called me and asked me to sit next to her, like she usually did when she had something important to discuss with me. She started, "I made a promise to you from the beginning that I was going to support you all I can to help you get an education. That promise still stands. You're one clever girl and you deserve all the support a mother can give, but we've gotten to a point where we have to make some sacrifices."

My mind started racing and all the negative connotations of a sacrifice started reeling before my eyes. *Sacrifices? Does that mean no school for me? What are we going to give up at this moment? Is Mom going to tell me to give up school and stay home?* At some point, she realized my mind wasn't there. I was with her physically but far away in my mental wanderings. She said, "Hey, listen to me." I returned from my wandering thoughts and listened.

She continued, "You can't go to Keta Secondary School. The odds are stacked against us. I can't sit here and leave you there in the hands of strangers. They might not handle you the way you ought to be handled. Again, I don't have the kind of money they are asking for right now. There's nowhere to go to ask for money. You'll have to give up Ketasco so you can go to a day school. That's cheaper and within our means and it also means I'll be closer to you to help and take care of you."

If a heartbreak came with a sound, mine would have been so deafening it would take hours to regain a sense of hearing. I felt shattered and disappointed, but I was also comforted by the fact that I wasn't giving up on school altogether. With the humility of a stray dog, I asked my mom, "What's the next step for me now? What school am I going to attend?" Everything my mom said led me to only one obvious choice. We lived in Agbozume. Agbozume had a day school. My mom wanted me to attend a day school where I would be closer to her. I wasn't good at math but this math was easy for me to do. The only choice left for me was

Agbozume Secondary School.

Mom confirmed my thinking, "We'll seek admission in Agbozume Secondary School. With your grades, they'll be happy to admit you." *I knew it!* I screamed in my head.

Mom sought admission for me the next day and I got it. Day school was supposed to be cheaper, but Mom still didn't have the money to pay for the things they required. That was when she decided to call on people—anyone at all—to lend her some money so she could to take me to school. It became difficult for her to get someone to lend her some money for my education. Money lenders at that time lent money to people organizing a huge funeral or fancy child outdooring, (a Ghanaian naming ceremony for a baby) but didn't see the need to lend money to a woman wanting to take her child to school, especially when the child was me: "crippled" and hardly useful.

At some point, my mommy got fed up with hearing no from all the people she had consulted for money. She was at her breaking point and looking for the next step to take. That was when one of her friends came to our house one dawn with an idea she thought would set my mom free from her suffering. That friend was called Atsudada, a woman who had twins and had not sent any of her children to school. Maybe, Atsudada didn't see the need, or she might have reasoned that spending money on children's education was a lost enterprise.

That morning, when she came around, my mom's spirit was somehow revived, thinking she was coming with some happy news, judging from the time she came to knock on our door. She told my mom, "I see you going up and down looking for money. People are laughing at you, and no one will lend you money to waste on a sick child. So, I've spoken to that seamstress at the edge of the road leading to the market. She has agreed to take your child as an apprentice. At least she could start putting thread in needles and later learn how to push thread into fabrics to sew dresses. She can be there as long as she wants, and even if she had to be there for the rest of her life, the seamstress wouldn't mind. That way, it gets the burden off your shoulders and your daughter can learn a trade instead of you moving from house to house begging people to give you money."

She was a friend and my mom had huge respect for the friendship. Mom thanked her and led her to the door for her to take her leave. You can't blame Atsudada for her perception of me. She had able sons and daughters and still had no reason to send them to school. You can't expect any good advice from such a fellow. She can only reason within her narrow horizon. It is then up to you to take her advice or not.

Mommy didn't give up. Early the next morning, she was at the door of one well-known money lender. She was so sure the man was going to help her because the man worshiped in the same church as my mom. The man didn't mince words when he told my mom the reason he couldn't lend her the money. "I lend money to farmers so they can pay me back after harvesting. Sometimes, the rains fail, and the seeds get corrupt—that's understandable. One day, the farmer will win again. Investing money in a child like yours doesn't look like something that will bring a win anytime soon. Sorry, I don't have money to waste on your daughter's education. Nothing good will come from it. Not now and not in the future."

This money lender was not alone in his perspective. A plethora of research has documented the detrimental effect violence, discrimination, and marginalization have on people with disabilities in Africa. The education systems established in Africa during the colonial period were rooted in ableist belief, patriarchal systems of rule, and perfectionist theories, hence the clear bias against people with disabilities. This especially affected women in school structure, curriculum, training of teachers, teaching and learning materials, teaching methods, and above all, the student assessment methods (UNICEF, 2018). These factors have presented massive challenges for people with disabilities who are too often hidden, considered useless or even thought of as cursed objects, leaving few opportunities for anything approaching a normal, self-supporting life.

There are only so many harsh words a woman can take for a day. I think it was at that point that my mom decided to stop moving from person to person for money and instead started looking for money within herself.

One afternoon, Mom placed her sewing machine on a table at the center of the room and started cleaning. Mom had the machine for a very long time but not once had I witnessed her cleaning it vigorously like the way she was doing that afternoon. I got curious; "Is someone coming to borrow the machine for work?" She said no, without lifting her head to look at my face. I asked again, "Are you taking it for repairs?" Again, she answered no without looking at my face. I kept quiet and looked at her as she busily cleaned the internals of the machine and oiled the moving parts with a soaked piece of cloth. I asked, one last time, "Where is the machine going?

This time around, she lifted her head up and looked at me. "I'm going to sell it. We've got fees to pay, and we have to pay it any way we can."

She left the house with the machine sitting on her head and came back without it. Another day, she gathered her new bedsheets, put them in a new cloth, and tied them. She left for town with the bedsheet in her armpit. She returned home that evening without the bedsheets. She had a piece of gold and silver that were given to her as part of her dowry. Traditionally, one is supposed to keep those treasures in the family for the next generation. That day, my mom gathered these things and left the house. Again, she returned without the gold and silver.

Mom wasn't alone in her efforts. I was also doing some petty trading by selling many different things in front of our house. Things like kerosene; fruits like oranges, bananas, and mango; charcoal, and pepper gum. I sold all these depending on the season.

One day she told me, "Get ready. Your uniform is with the seamstress and almost ready. You're starting school on Monday." I said to myself, "Finally, I will go to school, regardless of everything that has happened." Suddenly my heart was filled with this warm gratitude and happiness that made me forget about the disappointment of not attending my first-choice school.

CHAPTER 5 QUESTIONS:

–What things have you settled for when your first choice was not possible?

–What is non-negotiable for you when it comes to your education?

–How do we work to remove the barriers that prevent access? Do you think giving access removes barriers?

–What do accessibility, inclusion, and equity mean to you?

Chapter 6
The Road

It was three miles from our house to the Agbozume Secondary School campus. Obviously, I couldn't walk all that distance to and from school every day, so Mom had to look for ways to transport me to school. It wasn't an easy decision to take. Mom couldn't afford the services of a cab driver to take me to school and back every day. After much thought and consideration, she decided to buy a bicycle for a guy called John (who was also a first-year student who lived just opposite our house) to ride me to school and also bring me back home each day.

My first day riding on the back of the bicycle to school was a struggle. I had to learn how to balance myself on the bike with my crutches on my lap and school bag behind me. I also had to learn how to hold on tight to the rider when the going got tough. It was a rough stony road from my house to the school campus, so the goings and comings were always tough. We never had an easy ride. All through the ride, John kept reminding me to hold on tight to him or else I would fall off the bike and hurt myself. All my life I've learned to hold on tight to things. I've learned to hold on tight to the belief in myself and hold on tight to God as the provider of good things in my life. I've also learned to hold on tight to my education since it's the only way I could stand on the shoulders of giants and see the beauty of the world. I didn't know the day would come when I had to learn to literally hold on tight to a person. I did learn, and I was quick about it because, like the Humpty Dumpty, I didn't want to fall and break into pieces.

During the first day at school, I was told to go to a general arts class. During my days at Agbozume Secondary School, general arts students were considered the bright kids. Those who were not considered so bright were sent to other classes to learn agriculture or visual art. Being accepted in the general arts class added something to my confidence. I could walk with my head up high and scream to everyone who cared to listen that I'm a general arts student.

In the general arts class, apart from the core subjects, there were electives. For the electives, students were divided into two major combinations. One major was additional mathematics (or add mathematics) combined with geography and economics. The second major was purely languages – English, French and Ewe. When the time came for me to choose my electives, the school authorities themselves added me to the mathematics major. I didn't understand why they did that, but looking back, I believe someone saw my junior secondary school results and thought, "Sefakor is one smart girl. If she could make ten ones in the Basic Education Certificate Examination (BECE), she won't have any problem reading pure math, economics and geography." I didn't know much about these courses, but something within me said I could handle them without any stress.

When the bell rang for closing, I walked out to see my rider parked there patiently waiting for me. When he saw me, he came to me and helped me get onto the bike. Before he moved, he said, "Don't forget to hold on tight. It's a stony road, so it's going to be a rough ride." I held on tight to him with every strength I had in me, and very soon, we were back in the house.

It didn't take very long for me to realize how difficult my elective subjects were. I wasn't getting some of the economics concepts, but I was managing. Geography was okay until it got to the study of maps and latitudes. I started struggling there, too. Add mathematics brought the biggest challenge I had to deal with. The calculations started getting difficult and complex at every step of the way. No matter how keen I worked at it, I kept missing the point and kept getting every answer wrong. I followed the words of the teacher and watched every stroke of his chalk as he wrote on the board. It seemed okay, but if I was asked to solve a problem all by myself, I immediately began to have problems. But I wasn't going to give up that easily. I was determined to learn, make the grades, and make Mom proud of me. In fact, I did not know that I had Dyscalculia until I got to America and got diagnosed in 2012. Hmmm, issues of a broken system and invisible disability. I must say clearly that there are a lot of invisible disabilities that we do not have names for in our country due to so many reasons, and I will talk about that one day in another book.

Just as I was struggling academically, my bike also decided to develop some troubles of its own. One day on the road back home, John stopped abruptly and said, "Get down, the bicycle is spoilt. Let me see if I can fix it." For several minutes we stood there as he tried all he could to get the fault fixed. Several people passed us by. A few stopped to ask us what the problem was. He managed to get the fault fixed somehow, and we managed to ride it back home. From that day on, we always had to make a stop along the road to fix a fault before we could continue. If it's not a flat tire, it's a broken spoke or a faulty wheel, or a crank fault. Somedays I got to school late and missed some lessons. It got to a point where the bicycle couldn't work again. It got totally broken, so Mom had to negotiate with some people who had motorbikes so they'd bring me up to school and back.

That arrangement continued until Mom didn't have enough money to pay the bikers. Mom started owing them some arrears. The bikers complained, but she didn't have the money to pay them, so few months later, the bikers stopped coming to pick me up for school. Going to school each day became a struggle. I was left to find cheap and innovative ways to get to school and back each day. One day I had an idea. The trucks that were used to push goods to the market usually use the road leading to our school. If I could perch somewhere on the goods, then I could get to school every day for free.

One morning, I found myself on one of the trucks. The truck was loaded to its full capacity. It had boxes of fresh fish, baskets of onions, and other smelly goods. There was hardly a place for me to perch, but I tried all I could to squeeze myself in between the boxes of fish. Slowly, the truck got to my school junction and the pusher helped me to get down. I walked from the junction to the school campus. Anybody I met while walking to school walked past me and seconds later, turned back to watch me again. I didn't know why until I walked into the classroom. Almost all the students in the class turned to look at me. One asked, "Are you carrying a rotten fish in your bag?" That was when I realized why everyone I had walked past was looking back at me. I stayed too long in between the boxes of fish on the truck and began smelling like a fish.

I went through all these hustles to get to school, but I wasn't doing well in class. My electives were so hard that I had begun to lose interest in school, but anytime I thought of dropping out, Mom's voice echoed in my head; "If you want to reach up and touch the world, you'll need special support, and that support is your education. That's why you don't have to joke with it." I then decided to try harder, but no matter how hard I tried, my grades didn't improve. Rather, they got worse. Mom began to worry and that worried me a lot. My mom had a lot of worries on her own, so I shouldn't be the one to add to hers. If for nothing at all, I should be the one to bring smiles to her face. I woke up each morning, determined to turn my grades around, but my grades developed minds of their own.

I started getting sick. I developed a chronic migraine which took away my focus in class and made it very difficult for me to grasp what was being taught. The migraine got severe anytime I heard the word "mathematics." For instance, I could be very okay when we were doing a subject like social studies, which was one of the core subjects. When the lesson ended and I checked the school timetable to see that the next lesson was mathematics, the migraine began instantly. It became severe immediately when the mathematics teacher walked into the class. For two consecutive academic terms in my first year, this continued until I decided to change my elective subjects. I tried. God knows I did my best, but my best wasn't good enough to change my grades. So at the start of the third term, I moved to the languages class and began afresh.

It took me only one week to realize that I was in a place I should have been right from the start. The whole week I didn't experience any migraines. I had already fallen in love with the French language. Learning English felt like a breath of fresh air. Ewe was my mother tongue, so I didn't have any problem at all. I asked myself, "So what was I doing at that place of Mathematics when I could have been here right from the start?" Yes, I was enjoying lessons, but I had lost two terms of studies already and if I was going to do well, I would have to put in more effort than my peers. I didn't waste my break time playing or my free time engaging in unnecessary conversations. At break times, I went to friends and asked them to teach me the things I didn't know. In my free time, I went to some of the teachers to ask them questions and they answered.

French was a new language, so I had to do more if I was going to catch up. So Mom got our French teacher to give me extra classes after school. That wasn't enough. The gap between me and my peers was too wide, and it mostly had to do with the basics of French. If I was going to do well in the exams, I had to cover the basics first. So, during school vacations, Mom sent me over the Ghanaian border to French-speaking Togo to stay with her cousins who were living there so I could learn the language from scratch.

My first time in Togo, I started classes with children in kindergarten and first grade where we learned the alphabet in French and started basic sentence constructions. By the time I returned to Agbozume, my French had greatly improved. I wasn't only speaking the basics, but I was writing them correctly, too. My friends were amazed at the speed of my improvement. School was once again joyful for me. My spirit had been revived and I had come to enjoy my new progress.

Everything changed except the means I used to get to school. I was still boarding trucks and perching between foodstuffs. I was still going to school smelling like the food I perched between. Somedays, I went to school with a cocktail of scents—a little bit of fish smell here and a little bit of onion smell there. One day, on the way to write an exam, the truck I picked was carrying palm oil. I was so careful not to get to the exam hall with red palm oil stains, but it took only one bump of the truck to get the palm oil spilling all over my dress. I screamed, "Oh God, how do I go to school looking like that?" I didn't have the luxury of going back to change my dress, so I continued to school in that state. Some days I smelled like fish and some days I smelled like onions. That day, I didn't smell like any of those. I walked around looking oily and colorful like a missing piece of the rainbow.

CHAPTER 6 QUESTIONS:

- What obstacles (physical barriers to get to school, embarrassment, or shame) did you encounter in your journey to survive your early schooling and achieve your education goals?

- Are there accessible support systems in your country to help people with disabilities be more independent?

- As a change agent, can you think of some resources to help people with disabilities?

Chapter 7
Mount Mary

Everyone had a lofty dream of becoming something of worth when they were young. It's the way of the child to say something like, "lawyer," "president," or "engineer," when asked what they would like to be when they grow up. I had my own dream of becoming something; I wanted to become a television newscaster. The idea that the whole world would see me when I appeared on TV captivated my heart from a very young age. I wanted to prove a point, and being on TV could help me prove that point very easily. I wanted the whole world to know that it's not the end of the world when one loses their legs. They can work their way up to the TV for the world to see them. Deep down in my heart, I didn't forget what my dad did to me when I was young. I wanted to prove to him that I wasn't the finished case he thought I was. Being on TV could have been the easiest way to prove all that, but it's a crazy world we live in. Things change along the way and cause us to change too.

I don't know what changed, but along the line, I fell in love with different things, and those things guided my steps away from my initial dreams of becoming a newscaster.

I didn't have it easy going through the secondary school system, but through grit and perseverance, I was able to complete Agbozume Secondary School in 1993. When the results came, I had passed all the subjects except math. Without math, I couldn't go any further, so I had to re-sit (rewrite) and get a better grade before I could proceed to the tertiary level.

Students failing in one or two subjects wasn't just a local problem in 1993. It was a national problem. The government of that time sought to make changes in the educational system and that affected the number of years spent in pre-tertiary school and our preparation for the final exams. In an attempt to salvage the situation, the government of the day organized nationwide remedial classes at the regional and district levels so students who failed some papers could have an opportunity for a re-sit, with the cost covered by the government.

So, in 1994, some schools in southern Volta, including Agbozume Secondary School, had to camp at Akatsi Teacher Training College (Akatsico) to study and prepare for the retake of the failed subjects. I remember going to Akatsico and thinking about how I was going to live life while I was away from my mom. I got there and met some of my classmates who had also come to re-sit their failed papers. This made things easier. Also, I met some new people who went the extra length to help me have an easier life. One of these people was Wisdom.

Wisdom became like a brother to me, helping me every step of the way to ensure my safety around campus. Other friends even thought that we were cousins. When my mom brought food to me on campus, she made it for two, knowing very well that Wisdom will always be around me. Wisdom's mother also treated me the same way. Sometimes my mother brought shitor, which is hot black pepper sauce, and Wisdom's mother made abolo, dumplings and fried fish to complement it.

We were seen together all the time in group discussions with other students who were also having difficulty with the mathematics subject. We built a support system where friends could come together, discuss mathematics topics, and solve mathematics problems together. By the end of 1994, we wrote the exams, said our goodbyes, and left campus. We were so sure we were going to pass since we spent a lot of time learning, practicing, and answering past questions. In early 1995, our results were released, and I had a C in mathematics. It felt like I'd won the lottery that day. I was so happy and fulfilled that I could finally have a grade in mathematics that looked honorable enough to get me admission to the next level of my education.

Before my results came in, I'd already decided where to go. I had fallen in love with the French language and had decided to pursue it further at Mount Mary College. At that time, Mount Mary was the only training college in Ghana that trained professional French teachers. I had made up my mind to become a French teacher, so I applied for admission to Mount Mary. That year, over one thousand students applied to attend Mount Mary, and all did very well in French. An entrance exam had to be organized as they could select only two hundred brilliant students from the lot. It was a very traumatic experience for all of us involved. We all qualified to be given admission, but here we were being examined before being granted admission.

No one wanted to miss the chance of getting admission to Mount Mary, and not just because it's the only school that trained French teachers. It was also about the opportunity they offer to study abroad. Occasionally, students of Mount Mary were given the opportunity to travel to neighboring Francophonie countries and do a proficiency course in French. There were some instances where students traveled to France for such a proficiency course. This, and many other reasons, were why the entrance exams meant a lot more to each one of us than simply getting admission into a school.

I remember the night after the exams. All the students were gathered in front of the principal's office and names started being mentioned. They'll mention your name and tell you to stand on the left or the right side of the principal's office. All of us didn't know where we belonged until finally, the principal announced, "Those on my right are the ones who got admission into Mount Mary College. Those on my left, I wish you all the best in your next endeavors." I couldn't believe it when I realized I had gained admission into Mount Mary College. I screamed out of happiness and my happiness doubled when I realized that Wisdom, my brother from the Akatsico extra classes, had also gotten admission. I couldn't hold myself together, but I didn't fail to notice the hands of God in my selection. "What did I do to deserve this?" I asked myself. There were too many other people who were smarter than I am but didn't make the cut. If not for God who moved ahead of me, I couldn't have done it.

My feelings of joy and happiness suddenly disappeared when I saw the faces of friends who didn't make the cut. I know them and I know how much they wanted it, but they couldn't make it. Seeing their sad faces almost brought me to tears. I went to them, shared their disappointment, and offered them some words of encouragement. All was not lost. Most of these friends later had admissions into other tertiary institutions and most of them are doing very well in life now.

Mount Mary Teacher Training College of Education

Mount Mary sits on a hill that provides a rare opportunity to see the scattered buildings and trees of Somanya and Odumase townships. When you are on the campus at night and cast your eyes towards the township, all you see is darkness covering the buildings and trees and the piercing lights from the light bulbs installed in the various houses in the town. It's a beautiful sight to behold when you allow your mind to wander around, thinking about nothing but how light, no matter how little it is, can conquer the darkness of the night. These things cross your mind once in a while when you wander around the school campus at night, but during the day, life is busy. Everyone goes about their life, giving little attention to the view of the township and the kind of beauty it provides if one will only take the time to look at it.

The same thing that gave beauty to the school caused me most of my problems. A school on a hill looks graceful, but not to a person with a physical disability. You stand beneath the hill and cast your eyes up and the only question that springs up in your mind is, "How am I going to get there—to the top?" It came to mind the very first day I visited the school, but my mind was preoccupied with how to get admission into the school rather than thinking about my body's limitations. When I finally got admission into the school, that question took center stage in my thinking. I looked at the one hundred-plus stairs leading to the first-year classroom block and began to wonder, "How am I going to survive climbing all these stairs every day of my campus life?"

It wasn't easy for me, but I hadn't gone through all the trouble to gain admission only to give up because of the mountainous nature of the school. Whenever I got scared or troubled, the voice of my mother kept echoing in my head, "It's a very competitive world out there. You can't run; the world will always run and leave you behind. The only thing that can push you in front of this race is education." Once I remembered this, I told myself, "I'm ready to brave it all in order to get the education that I need, and nothing is going to stop me."

Many times, I was able to climb up the stairs to class without any trouble. Sometimes I got help from my mates and friends. Other times, I toppled over and fell. All it took was one misstep and I would fall and roll on the staircase until I got to the bottom of the stairs. I'd begin to climb again—that is if I did not get hurt or break anything. One morning, as I was climbing up the stairs, I lost balance, came tumbling down the stairs, and landed heavily at the foot of the flight of stairs. The fall was so heavy it broke my calipers and bent my crutches. I sustained a lot of injuries to my head and skin. I remember lying at the foot of the stairs and some mates rushing to my aid. They kept shouting for help, believing I might have sustained heavy injuries that would need instant medical care. That morning, they carried me into a car and sent me to Nsawam Orthopedic Center where I spent over a week receiving medical care and fixing my calipers so I could walk again.

That wasn't the last time I fell on the stairs. It happened many times. Some were severe and some led to minor injuries which didn't need hospital care. Every scar on my skin has a history and most of the history can be traced back to my time at Mount Mary. But my time at Mount Mary wasn't all about falls and injuries. It was also at Mount Mary that I discovered the true spirit of friendship and how far people with love in their hearts will go to prove their love for you. They don't say they love you. They act their love through the way they treat you and care for your needs. To date, anytime I think of friendship in its purest sense and color, Wisdom Akakpo, aka Azametuga or Tuga, comes to mind.

You will remember I first found him during our remedial days at Akatsico and he became the friend and the brother I needed during tough times. Somanya, the town where Mount Mary is located, is generally mountainous, and as a result, water was very scarce during our days there. People had to wake up early in the morning and walk a little over two miles to the town of Adjikpo to fetch water and cater to their needs. I wasn't in a position to do that trip daily to get water, obviously due to my disability. From day one, Tuga said to me, "Don't worry about that, I will help you." True to his words, he woke up very early to fetch water for himself and also for me. On weekends, he'd come for my laundry and take it to the riverside and wash it for me. When coming from the river, he would fetch water in a rubber bucket for me in one hand and fetch another bucket for himself, which he carried on his head. My washed clothes would hang from his shoulders as he walked the mile to deliver them to me.

Our mates made fun of him and questioned his intentions for doing so much for me, but it didn't bother him. All he did was go the extra mile to see a friend-turned-sister happy, and I was always thankful to God for bringing him my way.

As days went by at Mount Mary, I began to discover a lot about myself and learn new things every day. I discovered strength I didn't know I had and learned to do things I thought beyond me as a person with a disability. For the first time in my life, at age eighteen, I was separated from my mom and had to learn to live life all by myself. I had to do my morning chores all by myself without the help of anyone. The teachers in the school didn't think about my disability when there was work to be done. They treated me just like they did all other students and that helped me a lot. It changed my perception of people and made me feel like I belonged.

Physical education was something I thought was beyond me. In my mind, I said to myself, *I can't do this. It's too physical and demands the use of both legs and hands which I do not have.* So anytime we had PE on the timetable, I stayed behind, locked myself in the dormitory, and read something while my colleagues wasted away in the burning sun. One day, our PE tutor, Madam Mintah, reached out to me and asked, "Why do you stay away whenever we have PE?" I didn't answer that. In my mind, the answer should be obvious to her. She said, "You can't sit out my subject. You must get involved and learn whatever happens on the field because you'll be examined on it. Again, you can't treat yourself like you're different from all of us. Come out and get involved. If there's something you can't do, you can just sit and watch so you learn." Since that day, I always joined them on the field to take part in physical education. I did what I could do, and stayed out and watched while others did the things I couldn't do. In the end, I was grateful to be involved.

It was through these periods of involvement that I met a new friend who was just like me. She was also a person with a disability. Polio affected her right leg and she wore calipers just like me and walked with crutches just like me. Her name was Eunice Kotey, but everyone called her Copee. She was such an intelligent lady. She didn't like to talk. She preferred to express herself through academic work. There was no subject she wasn't good at. Talk about French, math, and all other subjects, and Copee will make all high marks. Because she didn't like to talk, people tried to pick on her. She remained quiet and took all the pain of embarrassment in, but I didn't allow that to happen. Once we became friends, I always got into trouble because of her. I would speak on her behalf and fight her fight for her.

Eunice was an introvert, but when you got closer to her, you'd know she was capable of all the fun you didn't associate with her. Behind the curtain of silence was a rap talent many people didn't know of. Copee was a talented rapper and could rap many Christian songs. Apart from that, she had a huge sense of humor which made me love her more. She was capable of making every serious situation look like play. I sat with her many times and asked her to teach me how to rap. That was when she taught me these rap lines, "We got to pray just to make it a day; that's why we pray." And the audience will respond "We pray, that's why we pray." This rap line became our anthem, and we formed a solid friendship that made the school refer to us as "the two musketeers."

During school entertainment, we would mount the stage and sing our rap song.

We became so popular that even when we were not ready to sing, they'd push us onto the stage and ask us to give them a rap. We took the microphone, started shouting the raps, and danced just to entertain the school. Anytime we mounted the stage, the whole crowd would go gaga, start laughing, and sing along with us. But we fell down a lot of times during those singing moments. The school stage was tiled and very slippery so our clutches couldn't give us proper balance. Copee would try a simple dance move and she would fall. I'd give her a hand to get up, but before I realized it, I was also down on the floor. Our falling down and getting up also became amusement they looked for whenever we were on stage. But we never stopped. We kept going and we kept falling down each time. We were happy to be on that stage, to feel part of the body of the school.

It's been so many years already, but I still remember those rapping days like it was only yesterday. Maybe it's because of the joy I found on the stage or because of the friend by my side. Either way, I always look back with a fulfilled heart knowing I'd found a sister and a friend who is still with me to this day. Copee is still a friend and occasionally, we talk on the phone, remembering all the fun we had while at Mount Mary College.

Mount Mary brought a huge positive change into my life. I went there to seek knowledge, but by the time I came home for the semester break, I realized a change of character in me. "Virtus et Scientia; Character and Knowledge," is the school's motto. It was when I passed through the system of training given to the people there that I realized the true meaning of the motto. At Mount Mary, it wasn't only about knowledge; it was also about character building. I came home looking at things differently. If I ever thought I couldn't live without my mother by my side, my time at Mount Mary changed that perspective. I could live a meaningful independent life if I'm allowed to. Yes, I needed friends sometimes, but largely I could do things for myself.

It was during my stay at Mount Mary that I found Mr. and Mrs. Atsu Mensah on campus, a couple I later came to stay with. I thought of them as part of my family because they also hailed from Agbozume and were both tutors on campus. I stayed with them during vacations and they took care of me as if I was their own child. When I needed certain things urgently on campus, they bought them for me and ensured that I was doing well in school. When fathers came to the school during visiting hours to visit their children, I felt the emptiness of not having a father figure in my life, who would also come around just as other fathers came around to visit. Mr. Atsu Mensah filled that space for me with his continuous care and concern during school visiting hours. I could show him off as my uncle and that vacuum was filled. Everybody knew on campus that he was my Mom's brother and therefore, my uncle. He was always there for me.

When we got to the final semester of the second year, we had to travel to Togo and stay there for six months as part of our study abroad program. This program was meant to ameliorate our French language in a French-speaking country so we can return with better proficiency in the language. Being in Togo previously, I found it easy to adapt to the learning culture of the country. When the study period was over, we came back to Ghana. It was after our return that I realized some Togolese refugees had come to live in our neighborhood. I got closer to a few of them and became friends with them so I could continuously speak the French language with them. They loved my learning spirit and tried as much as they could to correct me when I made a mistake with the speaking of the language and helped sharpen my French speaking skills.

Finally, in 1998, in my twenty-first year, we completed school and left the hilly grounds of Mount Mary. I went to the school as a young girl whose only possession was a dream to get an education so she could run with the world and not be left behind because of her disability. I went there with my mother's truth tucked in the corner of my heart, always urging me to go the extra mile for myself. I had God at the forefront of my mind, believing if I made him the center of my world, he would give me a deserved victory. Indeed, in the end, I had the victory that was promised.

There were hills that threatened my existence in the school as a person with a disability. There were hundreds of stairs I had to climb before going to class. I fell many times and spent many days at the hospital. There were people who were not nice to me and pushed me to the wall on many occasions. Teacher training was hard, especially for someone like me who had always lived her life relying heavily on the support of others. "But in all these things we overwhelmingly conquer through Him who loved us." (Romans 8:37). On the day I was leaving the campus, I looked back at the school on top of the hill one last time and said to myself, *These hills could not break me. Indeed, the Lord has been faithful.* He is a covenant keeping God, therefore, Deuteronomy 7:8 has been really fulfilled in my life.

CHAPTER 7 QUESTIONS:

–What does independence look like for you?

–What belief about your limitations is holding you back from achieving your goals?

–What is/are your identity/identities as a person and what makes you believe in it/them?

–Do you have people in your life who make the journey smooth for you despite all odds? Call them and say "Thank you for being in my life." It does not hurt but gratitude pays!

Our Wedding Day

My Sister Mawutor and I

Mum and I - Mama Josephine

My Siblings, Seyram and Selorm, with our Dad Rock

Training Teachers in my office at GES-Nswam

Prof. Geurts , Alex and I Advocating for the Rights to Information Bill

Paper Presentation at Basel - Switzerland

Friends in Denmark, Sandra & Louise

Presentation at IHCD in Boston

White Cane Awareness Day in Brattleboro

The State Dept. 2012 to Advocate for Disability Rights

Advocating for the UNCRPD at State Department in Washington DC

The State Department with David and Leah

Judy Heauman & I

The International Alliance of Women - TIAW Award - Washington DC

When I met the motivational Speaker Pastor Nick Vujicic - San Francisco

I was giving a commencement speech during our graduation at SIT - Vermont

Campaigning for Disability Rights

The Twins

My SIT Policy and Advocacy Classmates and Our Professor Jeff Unsicker

Chapter 8
The French Teacher

I left college with one unanswered question on my mind: Where am I going to start my teaching profession? I knew where I wanted to go, but the power to be there wasn't altogether in my hands. After teacher training college, students are given the opportunity to choose the district they want to be posted at. You chose the district and leave the rest of the placement to the authorities. At first, I wanted to start my teaching profession in Agbozume, where I would be closer to my mom and also have the opportunity to serve in the community where I grew up, but the teachers in Mount Mary drew my attention to one important thing I had overlooked: access to healthcare. They said, "You've spent a lot of time going in and out of Nsawam Orthopedic Center due to your condition. You fall. You break down. Wouldn't it be prudent if you chose a school in Nsawam where you'll be closer to the orthopedic center?"

A spark lit up in my head. I asked, "Why didn't I think about this earlier?" So, from that day on, I made it a point to get posted to Nsawam instead of Agbozume. The process wasn't easy. After selecting Eastern Region where Nsawam is located, I had to do a follow-up every now and then to ensure that I would actually be posted there. I went to the regional office in Koforidua on several occasions to make a case. I told them, "I'm a person with a disability and have very specific physical needs. I would be very glad if you posted me to Nsawam where I would be able to access quick healthcare when the need arises." My situation didn't convince them. The man in charge argued with me, "You're asking us to do what we ought not to do. You want to be favored but the system doesn't play favoritism when it comes to teacher placement. Also, you're not the only teacher with special needs, so why should we favor you and leave the rest?"

That didn't stop me from seeking what was right for me. Others might not find reasons to pursue what is due them, but that shouldn't stop those of us who are ready and willing to pursue what's right for us. I went there on several occasions, bearing letters from doctors and from Mount Mary administrators confirming my situation. I still didn't receive any positive feedback from them. I stopped pursuing it until the postings were released. That was when I realized that my effort wasn't in vain. I was posted to Nana Osae Djan School, a junior secondary school, at Nsawam in the Eastern Region of Ghana. The joy I felt that day could not be described in words. I gave up the pursuit but God came through for me, as He always did. My happiness doubled when I later found out that my school mother from Mount Mary was also posted to the same school. *God has a sneaky way of sending help ahead to the places He desired for me, I thought to myself.* Jeremiah 29:11 was at play strongly: "For I know the thoughts that I think toward you, saith the LORD, thoughts of peace, and not of evil, to give you an expected end."

I left home in September of 1998 to begin my teaching career in Nsawam. It was Mavis, my school mother, who helped me secure housing in Nsawam. She said, "You don't need to be far from the school. The terrain isn't good for your movement. We'll find somewhere closer to the school where you won't have to walk a far distance to the school premises." True to her words, she found me a place very close to the school. Able people took five to ten minutes to walk from there to the school premises. It took a little over twenty minutes to walk to the school, but that was okay. It was the closest I could get.

When I needed someone to show me around the school, it was Mavis who did. She walked next to me while we talked about our time on campus and what it felt like to teach in Osae Djan. She said, "This is one of the best schools in this area, so much is expected from the teachers here. You can't be lazy and you can't give half of what you know. You're always required to give one hundred percent and nothing less. You see the kids around here? They are the sons and daughters of highly placed individuals in the public sector like doctors, police, and prison officers. You can't afford to let them down."

Everything Mavis told me became evident on the very first day I went to the class to teach. The kids were very excited about learning and kept asking questions whenever they didn't understand something. Teachers didn't allow you to eat into their lesson times. Immediately after the bell tolled for lesson change, you'd see the next teacher standing at the door of the class signaling you to end your lessons. Everything was perfectly structured for learning to take place at a speed the kids were comfortable with.

On my first day in class, I told the kids, "I'm going to teach the French language. Yes, it's just like any other subject you do here, but it will benefit you a lot if you treat it as learning a new language. You can learn a new language if only you're ready to speak it. So, during my lessons, each and every one of you will speak only French. You'll make mistakes and I'll be here to correct you. You'll interact with your friends in French too. That way, we all will grasp the language quickly and make good use of it." They chorused; "Yeees, Madam!"

I was surprised by their effort and curiosity to learn the language. When there was a word they didn't understand, they'd run to me for an explanation. Those who were quick to learn offered to help those who struggled. In my classes, no one was scared to make a mistake, knowing very well that they would be corrected when they made one. Not too long afterward, these kids started making simple sentences in French. It wasn't perfect, but it was a good start. If the word sounded funny, they laughed about it, but in the end, they learned to use that word correctly. One significant word that sounded funny and was always used before the school closed was heureuse, which means happy. They ended up giving me the nickname *Madame Heureuse* which carried through the years. I was always in their midst, mentoring them, correcting them, and encouraging them to speak up and write the right way. I really enjoyed teaching at Nana Osae Djan School.

In 1999, the first batch of French students Mavis and I taught sat for the BECE, and when their results came, ten students had ten ones. It had never happened in the school's history that ten students had ones in all ten subjects, especially in French. That threw the whole student population into jubilation. They gathered and ran around town amidst drumming and dancing. They kept singing my name, "Madam Sefakor abɛ yɛ biooo..." (This is the doing of Madam Sefakor). Truth be told, I wasn't the only one responsible for such a feat. By the time the results came, Mavis, who also taught that batch French, had left the school to pursue further studies. I was the only one available, so they showered all the credit on me.

A lot of things changed for me during my second year in the school due to the success of the first batch. Parents from other schools came asking me to start classes for their wards. They were so sure I was going to make an impact in the lives of their kids if I took them through some extra lessons in French. That was the point I decided to run extra classes for kids at a small fee. Schools closed at 2 pm and we ran a two-hour extra class for students and closed at 4 pm. My classes started at 5 pm and closed at 7 pm. It wasn't only for students of Osae Djan. Students from other schools were allowed to join.

The following year, students who sat for the BECE did very well in French. Even students who didn't attend Osae Djan but only attended my extra classes made high scores in French. The publicity of the French classes continued growing as students started spreading the good news through word of mouth. Eventually, the classes became so large that I started running more sessions. I had over a hundred form one students and about ninety form two students. Form three students were also running close to one hundred as well. These large numbers brought about some small trading opportunities. I sold homemade ice cream to those who wanted it and sold chilled sachet water to students who needed it.

The money realized from these ventures kept me going. I remember at one point I didn't need to touch my salary because I was making enough money from the extra classes and items I was selling to the students. I saved most of the money and reinvested some of the money into other ventures. I ventured into buying and selling when I realized there was an opportunity to make more money from that. I bought copper jewelry and hitarget fabrics from Togo and sold them to staff and people in the community for a little profit.

When the time came for me to go back to school, I didn't have a problem with finances because I had saved enough to help me further my education. After four years of hard work and mentoring kids to aspire to be more, I finally decided it was time for me to go. Teaching, for me, wasn't just a job. I didn't have to wake up each morning, go to class, and push chalk on the blackboard so I could call myself a teacher. It was a call, a call I answered with the aim to make every child who passed through my hands better than I found them. If I was to give an account on the work I did in Osae Djan today, I would be proud to say that most of the kids that passed through my hands are in better places. I can point to lawyers, doctors, politicians, and great teachers of the French language and say, "These are the products of my work at Osae Djan from 1998 to 2002."

CHAPTER 8 QUESTIONS:

–There is an African saying, "Where determination exists, failure cannot dismantle the reign/flag of success." What role does determination play in your life?

–What is disability pride to you?

–Do you think Persons with Disabilities (PWDs) should have any pride at all? As you can see, I am not just a teacher but a French Language Teacher which is my pride.

–How do you own your identity amid systemic or ableist structures and barriers?

– What steps can you take to make your life and the lives of others a bit more comfortable and fulfilling?

–You have to make that choice even in the midst of the storm with so many barriers.

Chapter 9
Love of a Man

One day, after a Ghana National Association of Teachers (GNAT) meeting, a gentleman walked up to me and said "Hello." I looked to his face and responded, "Hello." He asked if I knew him. I looked at him closely but couldn't recall where I had met him. I told him, "Please help me recall." He said, "Two years ago, my family and I attended a funeral service at Agbozume. We went to eat at a friend's house. That was where I saw you. Coincidentally, you lived in the same house we came to visit." Mentioning the name Sena struck a chord and I immediately remembered the occasion he described very well. He spoke my language and had a name that belonged to my tribesmen.

He attended Jasikan Training College and was posted to Damang, one of the villages near Nsawam. One thing about the Ewes: when we meet in a place far from home, we become automatic siblings. In my language, we call it Nyebro—"My brother and sister," so from that day on, he became my brother. Our friendship started from taking pictures at programs, cooking and washing together with friends, and even doing church work together. Bubu was so helpful and very industrious that we took our friendship to the next level of doing business together. We bought goats cheaply from Damang and he helped me get someone to rear them. We later ventured into buying and selling maize. We bought maize, hoarded it until it became scarce, and sold it for a higher margin. We made some money together and later bought a taxi for business and as a way to transport ourselves.

In my mind, we were building a relationship beneficial for both of us, but Bubu didn't think the same way. He had another motive that was larger than what I thought we could be. One day after a GNAT meeting, he approached me with two other friends. He said, "I was wondering if my friends and I could walk you home." I looked at him and his two other male friends (Tizo and Akah). They too spoke Ewe, so it felt like a meeting between tribesmen. I answered, "Why not?" The three of them followed me home. We cooked and ate and shared our experiences about the community we found ourselves in.

The four of us formed a family, or so I thought. One day, the texture of the relationship changed. I blame it on Bubu. We were just friends going about our work and sharing moments of happiness together until he walked up to me and said, "Sefakor, I love you and I want you to be my wife." I didn't know how to feel when he said that, but one thing was for sure. I felt very disappointed. "Ah Bubu, why would you say that? We are friends, isn't that enough for you?" My disappointment escalated to anger when he kept saying, "I don't only love you. I want you to be my wife."

Growing up, I looked at love and relationships through the lens of my mother. She told me, "Don't go around listening to boys who say they love you. There's no true love in a man. If there was, your father would have been your first true love, but where is he now? Concentrate on your books and look up to God for your daily sustenance. Don't give your heart to men. They'll break it into pieces." So that day, I decided to cut Bubu out of my life. I didn't want to see him again and I didn't want to hear from him again. If it was love he wanted, he should hit the street and find one and leave me alone.

But that guy didn't know how to stop. He kept coming and coming until one day, out of frustration, I told him, "If it's me you want, then go and talk to my mother." I said that to bring closure to the topic as I knew very well that Bubu couldn't go to my mom and say the things he said to me.

When school vacated, I went back home to my mother as I always did on every vacation. The whole family had finished eating and relaxing under the mango tree in front of the house when we heard a knock on the gate. Three gentlemen walked in; It was Bubu and his two other friends. I was shocked when I saw them. *How did they get here? Who showed them where I live and what in the name of hell are they doing here?* As I was busily battling with these questions in my head, my mother's demeanor was quiet and assuring. It looked like she knew something I didn't know. She offered them a seat and they sat down.

Before they could utter a word, I retorted, "What are you guys doing here?" But my mom insisted that the right procedure had to be followed. We offered them water as the Ewe custom demanded, and my mom later asked, "What brought you gentlemen here today?" Bubu answered, "We are here today because of what we discussed the other time."

The other time? What other time? I asked in my mind. Everything looked so strange to me. I couldn't understand how they were able to locate my house because we'd moved from the place where he'd first seen me. To make matters worse, they were talking about "the last time." What last time? My mom might have sensed the frustration in my mind and decided to set me free from my own confusion. She said, "Bubu was here the other time while you were in school. He came to tell me about his intentions towards you. He said he loves you and wants to make you his wife. I'm your mother but I can't decide for you in matters like this, so I told him to go and come back at a time when you are home with me. That's why they are here today. Most importantly, I asked him to think about what he said carefully and be sure of his decision before coming back to meet us. Today, he's here. Let's listen to what he brought."

Bubu repeated everything he had already told me. Mom asked, "Are you sure of what you are saying? As you can see, Sefakor is physically disabled and cannot compete with other girls." He answered, "Yes, I'm sure and really want to marry her. I can imagine all the obstacles ahead, but I am convinced she is the love of my heart." At this point, I was dumbfounded. It felt like I'd been pushed into the middle of a drama and forced to act along. My mom told them, "It's ok, leave the rest to me. I'll talk to Sefakor and make sure she accepts your proposal." That was the point Bubu decided to take the drama a few notches higher. He dipped his hand into his pocket and brought out a ring. I was just sitting there watching him in awe. He knelt before me and said, "Sefakor, I love you and want you to marry me. Will you be my wife?"

At this point, I was too overwhelmed to say no. I looked at him and nodded shyly in affirmation. That was 2001, a year before I left Osae Djan for the University of Cape Coast. I wore my promise ring in the presence of my family.

Meeting with My Father

Going to look for my father was never on the agenda for me. He never looked for us since the day he dropped that letter and left. Mom moved on, got married, and began a new family with this lovely man who had become my dad. I had moved on too. All I had of him were memories of times when I was young and he cared, but anytime I thought of how he left me and Mom in the lurch, my heart began to hurt. It was a memory I didn't visit often due to how it made me feel, but when the love between me and Bubu pushed us to the altar, the question became: On your wedding day, which of your fathers will give your hand away in marriage as our Ewe culture demands?

To me, it was a straight answer: "My step-dad." He had been there since I was ten or eleven years old. He had been the father figure in my life, so he deserved the honor to hold my hand on that day and give me away as our tradition demands. Our pastor didn't agree with me. He said, "As long as your biological father is alive, tradition requires that he gives your hand away in marriage. Not a step-dad." I screamed, "Oh no! That shouldn't be the case." The pastor said, "Don't look at the hurt he caused you. Give him what's due him."

Honestly, it was very hard for me and my mom. Bringing my father into my wedding plans was like bringing the old devil back from his hiding place. I didn't want that, but I had to learn to forgive as a fervent Christian does. Life becomes a field of light when the one who is hurt learns to forgive. That way, she welcomes the one who hurt her back into the light of God so both can dwell. I went through six months of counseling to learn to forgive my father. In the end, I prayed, "And forgive us our trespasses, as we forgive those who trespass against us."

I set off to look for my father.

I spoke to my uncle, my father's junior brother who was there right from the beginning. I told him, "I want to meet my father to discuss my impending marriage with him. I don't want to call him before I go there, so kindly speak to him and enquire about his availability and schedules so I know when he will be home." Some days later, he got back to me with all the information about my father's whereabouts and when I could meet him at the house. He lived in the police quarters in Tema, not far from Accra. My uncle took me to have a look at the house in which my father lived so I could go alone whenever I was ready to meet him.

On that day, I went with Bubu. When we got to his house in Tema, we met a lady who said, "Chief Inspector Komabu is at work, but he should be home any moment now." She gave us a place to sit in the sitting room. There was a table in front of the chair, so when I sat in the chair, I pushed my legs and crutches beneath the table. At some point, Bubu had a call on his phone and left the room to receive it outside. Not too long afterward, we heard footsteps approaching the sitting room. It was my father. He must have seen me when he was about to enter the sitting room. I overhead him asking the lady, "Who's that beautiful friend of yours?" The lady responded, "I don't know her. She came with a gentleman to look for you."

My dad entered the room and came to sit on the opposite side of the table, face to face. Bubu also entered the room right after my dad and came to sit next to me. My dad looked at us and smiled. He asked, "What case brought you here this afternoon?" In his mind, we had come to his house to seek his help concerning a police case. I told him, "Dad, this is Sefakor. We didn't come here because of a police case. We came to see you." He sat slack-jawed with surprise in his eyes. "Sefakor?" he asked. He bent down to look at my legs beneath the table. When he raised his head again, he couldn't look at me in the eyes. He sat there wearing an expression of guilt and confusion. I looked at him very well. Age had caught up with him, but he was still a very handsome man.

I told him the reason we had come to see him; "Dad, this gentleman next to me is Bubu. He and I are getting married soon and we have come to inform you so that on that day, you'll hold my hand and give me away as our custom demands." He still couldn't shake the guilt and shame, so he spoke to me while his eyes wandered around the room. He said, "Dowry belongs to fathers who have been present in their daughters' lives and have taken responsibility for their upbringing. As you're aware, I wasn't present, and I wasn't responsible. I've had no hand in what you've grown up to become. I, therefore, lack the right to even be present at your wedding, let alone receive your dowry as a father. I don't even know how I'm going to survive in the midst of your mother's family, knowing everything that happened. I know what shame looks like and I don't dare to come around on that day, but because you have given me that respect and recognition, I will also honor you. I will appoint my junior brother, your uncle Korsi, to be there in my stead."

He spoke like a man who knew the consequences of his actions and wouldn't like to do anything to change what should befall him due to his actions and inactions. He handed me over to my uncle Korsi, and from that day on, we planned everything concerning the marriage with my uncle. He was very clear on the role he had to play, and we kept him in the loop so that at any point in time, he knew what was happening concerning the marriage arrangement.

The Marriage

There were so many people who questioned, "Why would an able gentleman choose to marry a woman with a disability? Aren't there other women around who are more beautiful and more deserving of a marriage than this one?" Such questions never stopped coming, and you'll be surprised to hear the caliber of people who asked such a question. You may think of them as people who should have known better, but it wasn't all together their fault. Their reason for asking such a question came from the way they were brought up and the lens through which they were made to look at disability. They were brought up to see a person with a disability as shameful. Culturally, people with disabilities were pushed behind the curtains where no one can see them. If a family had a person with a disability, the whole family was considered cursed. In their minds, people with a disability should not win, not because they cannot, but because their culture says so.

When our wedding date got closer, I remember my aunt calling me on the side and asking, "Fakor, think about this again. Your mother had been there before, and you shouldn't have to go through the same struggle. From deep down in your heart, do you believe this man loves you? Do you believe his love for you is genuine?" She might have asked that question from a place of love and care for me, but why did she doubt the love Bubu had for me? Would she have asked the same question if I wasn't a woman with a disability?

All these questions made me decide to make a statement during my wedding, a statement that sought to change the narratives surrounding people with disabilities. I told Bubu, "I don't just want to be married traditionally; I would like to have a white wedding in the presence of God and friends in the chapel after our traditional one. I don't want to do the wedding in my hometown. Let's do it in the capital where the world can see a woman with a disability getting wedded." He agreed, "I'm behind you on this. Let's do it." Yes, can't keep calm at all!

So, we had our traditional marriage on the 5th of July, 2003. On the 6th of July, I wore my wedding dress, put my makeup on, and readied to walk the aisle in the Global Evangelical Church, Tesano-Accra branch. My uncle Korsi was present as planned. He held my hand, walked down the aisle, and presented me to my husband, who was already waiting for me in the church. We exchanged our vows amidst cheers and jubilation. He looked into my eyes and said, "I do." I looked into his eyes and promised him my eternal love. The pastor declared, "I pronounce you husband and wife," and from that day on, we've been nothing short of what the pastor declared in our lives.

It was a beautiful day for us, looking at all the people present and all the love we received. The wedding got people talking. Those who didn't believe when they heard it came to witness it with their own eyes and sent the message forward. I felt very fulfilled when I realized that the Agenda Newspaper had covered our wedding. My goal to change the narrative and present a new story of victory for people with disabilities was achieved. I will tell you more about my love and marital life in the next book. Don't let me forget.

CHAPTER 9 QUESTIONS:

−In your perspective, what does it mean to be loved?

−Do you think people with disabilities also have the rights and feelings necessary to get married?

−Are there any cultural practices that prevent you from engaging and being fully included in life events?

−Through whose lens do you see love and marriage?

−Your parents' lens or your own lens?

Chapter 10
University of Cape Coast

There was pride in my heart from the very day I stepped foot on the soil of the University of Cape Coast (UCC). I knew it was one step closer to the fulfillment of a dream—a dream my mother placed on my heart from the beginning of my journey. What she told me rang a bell in my ears as I stood still looking around the campus: "Sefakor, if you want to reach up and touch the world, you'll need special support, and that support is your education." Remembering her voice and what she said to me that day put a smile on my face. I looked at her beside me and smiled. She was with me on that very day as we walked toward the school's administration block to sort out my accommodation.

From the beginning, it looked impossible. It didn't make sense to a lot of people who saw me seated behind a bicycle on my way to school, but there I was, on the soil of one of Ghana's most prestigious universities for higher education. I looked around to observe the environment in which I was going to spend the next four years of my life. People—a lot of people—kept walking up and down looking for things I did not know. Some walked in groups and others walked in pairs. I looked at faces and said hello to some of them. They smiled and said hello to me, too. It felt like home, especially seeing all those beautiful people around.

I looked at the tall, storied buildings surrounding me and said to myself, "Stairs, it looks like you and I can't part forever. You're with me every step of the way." I scanned around the campus where I was standing and there was no single building that had special access for people with disability. Not that I expected to see access for people with disability all around the campus, but somewhere at the corner of my heart, I hoped to see something that said, "We don't have it all, but we are trying." I didn't see anything of that sort. I wasn't afraid, but that didn't stop me from thinking about all the bad times I've had with stairs in the past.

I looked at my admission letter again to be sure of the hall I was allocated to. "Atlantic Hall," it stated. It was when we got to the room I was allocated to that the authorities realized I was a person with a disability. The man there said to me, "In Atlantic, women go to the top floor of the hall while men live on the ground floor." I told him, "Look at my condition. It doesn't look like a good idea for me to live on the top floor." He said to me, "It's the hall's policy. I didn't make the policy." There was a little exchange of words here and there until Dr. Quist, who was then the Hall Master, came in. He said, "Young woman, kindly give us some time to resolve this. We will get back to you soon."

All day, I stood outside with my luggage and other belongings waiting for them to decide on where to place me. Finally, they decided to take me to Adehye Hall, an all-female hall of residence that was located on the southern campus, just like Atlantic Hall. They placed a call to the Hall Mistress of Adehye Hall to inquire about the possibility of a swap, and she told them, "That can't be possible. All arrangements concerning allocations had already been done. Bringing a new student here will cause a huge distraction to the whole arrangement." We were all left standing there, not knowing what to do next. That was when Dr. Kafui Etsey, a man I had known from our church, came in and said, "It looks like the hall authorities will need some time to resolve this issue. Let me take you home with me as they try to figure out how to resolve the issue."

After a week at Dr. Etsey's bungalow, the hall authorities reached an agreement to keep me on the ground floor of Atlantic Hall. On the very day that the news came, I packed my things and went to Atlantic Hall, Room 126, where I was assigned. Atlantic Hall was a five-floor building where each floor has one washroom containing two toilet cubicles and two-bathroom cubicles. When I was placed on the ground floor with the gentlemen, we wondered how I was going to share the washroom with them, but the men were kind and considerate enough to leave the washroom and its accessories for my sole usage. They woke up each morning, climbed up to the next floor, and used the washrooms there. Each time any of them needed to use the washrooms, they had to go up and use the ones there. So, for the next four years of my life on campus, I stayed among the men on the ground floor, in the same room with a friend, Room 126, and had the washroom on the ground floor to myself.

◊

As first-year students, we needed to register for our school ID cards. This took place in front of the school's administration block, and all first-year students were required to gather in front of the administration block to register. I went there early in the morning, but the queue was already formed, and there were over a hundred students ahead of me. That meant I had to stay in the queue for hours until my turn. Some students came around, saw how long the queue was, and left, but I was determined to get my ID that very day so that I could move on to other things that were required of me. At one point, I couldn't bear the pain of fatigue that I was going through. I only had one leg to stand on and that leg was already tired. Then I heard the lady standing right in front of me talking on the phone. She was speaking Ewe —the variant from parts of Togo. I said in my head, "This is one of my people." When she hung up the phone, I tapped on her shoulder and spoke Ewe to her, "I've been here for hours and I'm tired already. Could you please allow me to take your place when it gets to your turn?"

She looked at me, obviously thinking about my situation, and said, "No problem at all." She left the queue for some minutes and when she returned, she told me, "I've been looking for a chair for you to sit on but couldn't find any. There's this rock I found there [she pointed to the location] you can sit on the rock and wait, and when it's my turn, I'll call you to register." She gave me a helping hand and walked me to the rock. I sat there and waited. About an hour later, she came back to call me. "It's your turn now, get up and let's go." She helped me to the place of registration, and I got registered. After my registration, I stayed behind and waited for her to finish hers so I could say thank you.

When she finished her registration, we started talking about ourselves and where each of us came from. We had lunch together that day and talked more about our lives and the courses we had come to study at UCC. That was when I learned she was called Mawuto without the "R", and she was at UCC to do the same course that I was doing. From that day, we became inseparable friends. I told her for the sake of the Anlo Ewe, I will write her name with the "R" at the end. I must say that Mawutor is a very calm, quiet, and clean lady and I am the direct opposite. After all, I have spent all my life crawling on the ground, so I know what we call noise and dirt. In short, I am a waterstone who knows no cold. As you can see, she is my angel.

In Mawutor, I found a sister I could talk to about my challenges and fears. It was with Mawutor I discussed my challenges. I told her, "The greatest challenge I've ever faced in my academic life wasn't with academic work itself. It always has to do with stairs—staircases and how to climb them safely to attend classes. Sometimes I fall. Most often when I fall, I get up, dust myself off, and continue climbing. Or on a good day, friends come to my aid. But there are times that the fall is too hard, I hurt myself, and spend days in the hospital." She answered, "Unfortunately things are not any better around here. All of our lectures are going to be on the top floors of the lecture hall. What are we going to do about it?" I told her, "I always manage. This too, I'll manage."

The first-year communication skills lecture was at the Science Roof Top (SRT), a building that had three stories. Mawutor looked at me and asked, "What are we going to do?" After several minutes of brainstorming, we agreed that since SRT was too high, she would attend the lectures and take notes. In the evening, she would teach me whatever was taught. This arrangement continued for weeks, but eventually, I felt that I was missing a lot. It's different when you are in the lecture room being lectured. Apart from listening to what the lecturer would say, there's the added advantage of asking questions and listening to the opinions of other students on the subject. I was missing the whole lecture hall experience and I wasn't happy about it.

I decided to start attending the lectures myself. Sometimes, friends carried me on their backs and took me to the lecture hall. Other times, I wrapped my right arm around the shoulders of a friend and wrapped the left one around the shoulders of another and I hung between the two as they carried me over the stairs to the classroom block. Most lecturers saw me being carried to the class and said nothing or did nothing about it. They saw it as a clever and fun way to get around obstacles. I knew that no one was going to change my situation for me if I sat down and did nothing. I couldn't see myself going through all that hustle every day for the rest of my four years on campus. I knew I had to do something for a change, but where was I going to start?

My shoulders began hurting from all the times I had to hang around people's necks, literally, to be carried to class. My knees began hurting from all the times I had to climb the stairs myself. Sometimes I walked up to the staircase and looked to my left and to my right to check if there was anybody around to help me. There would be no one. I would stand beneath the staircase and count all the stairs I had to climb before getting to the classroom. It became daunting and I had no strength left to do it, so I walked back to my room and slept with a broken heart.

One morning, I went to the office of our Communication Skills (CS) Chair and made a case for my situation on campus. He listened to me attentively, the way people who are interested in what you're saying listen to you. I thought I was making an impact. I saw the look on his face while he listened to me. It was that of concern and empathy. I believed him to at least make an effort to change things for me, but after listening to my lamentations he said, "I'm impressed by your boldness to walk up to me and seek a solution to your problem, but the sad thing is, I can't do anything about it. The stairs are already there, and I can't unmake them."

I was heartbroken, but I wasn't going to give up just yet. I told him, "I know what we can do. The only thing I need is one with the power to make it work. There is one class that happens on the ground floor. The class starts and finishes at the same time as mine. I've checked into the class and saw no person with a physical disability there, but I'm a person with a physical disability and my class is on the top floor. Why don't we swap these classrooms, so my class comes down to the ground floor and makes it easier for me to attend?"

I thought that was the easiest way to solve a nagging problem that has become a threat to my safety on campus. The CS Chair looked into my face and said, "Again, I'm impressed with your boldness, but I can't help it. You can't just get up and swap venues for lectures. There are a lot of internal politics involved and I'm not ready to go through that. I'm sorry, but I can't do anything about it." I said thank you to him and left his office. I had grown so frustrated that nothing was going to stop me from seeking the help I needed to solve the problem. He said he couldn't help me, but I thought to myself, *just because he can't help me doesn't mean no one can. I'll move on to the next person until I find help.*

The next person I went to was the lecturer on the ground floor whose lecture coincided with mine. She was a beautiful young woman who had just been employed as a history lecturer. I told her my situation. I gave her reasons for why it would be easy for her to swap the class. She asked me, "Have you spoken to anyone about your situation?" I answered, "Yes, I've spoken to our CS Chair. He said he couldn't do anything about it, but I trust you. If you agree to swap, it would be easy for my class to do the same." Her demeanor was of someone who'd love to help if you could judge from how sweet her voice was when she spoke to me.

"I haven't been here for so long and I don't think I'm in a position to make that decision. I'm only a lecturer. If your CS Chair says he can't do anything about it, then I'm the last person you can expect to change things. I admire your bravery, going all this length to seek a solution to your problem. I wish I could help."

My face fell when I realized that the two people I believed could help me couldn't help. For the rest of my stay on campus, I spoke to many individuals in authority hoping to get them to make a change, but all of them gave me the same line, "There's nothing I can do about it." One day I spoke to an old lecturer about this same situation, and he said to me, "Climbing up here is the only exercise I do, so I don't want my lectures on the ground floor. Use it as a form of exercise too. It won't kill you." One also told me, "We can't swap lecture halls just because of you. We don't have to inconvenience everyone just because of you and your comfort." No one saw the situation as urgent because I was the only person on campus who had a physical disability, but the question is, how many of us did they need before they would make a change?

◊

When I got to the second year, I got myself a scooter. That scooter belonged to a woman with a disability who had died. When the woman died, her children decided to sell the scooter to anyone who offered the right amount. My mom got a hint of it and impressed upon me to buy it. After learning about how the scooter operated, I fell in love with it and decided to buy it. The scooter helped my mobility a lot but it didn't solve the vertical mobility problems I was going through. Each morning, I charged it until the battery was full, tucked my crutches on the side, and drove off. When I got to spaces the scooter couldn't enter, I used the crutches to continue with the journey.

In my third year, I was still climbing stairs to attend lectures. By that time, I'd become very well-known on campus, so people were ready to offer help whenever I needed it. They continued carrying me on their backs and shoulders to classrooms. Though it was very uncomfortable and sometimes unsettling, I'd grown used to it. In our third year, they brought a man to Atlantic Hall who was blind. He was also given a room on the top floor, but after some discussions were made, they agreed to bring him to the ground floor. When he came, I gave him the extra bathroom and the toilet that was left unused since I came there. I had a discussion with him, and he expressed the same access problems.

One day, during a chat with Mawutor, I remembered an incident that happened after our matriculation. I remembered after the matriculation, when the lecturers were marching out from the podium, the Vice Chancellor Professor Addo-Obeng tapped my shoulder and said, "I hope your accommodation issue is settled now, and I believe you're enjoying your stay here?" I remember after the matriculation, I told Mawutor what the VC said and Mawutor went like, "Eiii the VC knows you? Then you're popular, ooo." We both burst into loud laughter. When the memory of that incident came to mind after some months, I said to Mawutor, "The VC already has an idea about me, so I'm going to write a letter to him and see if something can be done about the problems people with disabilities go through on campus."

That day, I took a pen and paper and wrote a letter enumerating all the problems people with disabilities face on campus. I sent the letter to the VC and waited for his response. I was only relying on hope to get a response from him. In my mind, the VC had other more pressing issues to attend to than responding to a letter from a random student seeking his attention. Two or three days later, I got a letter. I opened it and it was a letter from the VC. I couldn't hold myself together. At that moment, the content of the letter didn't matter to me. I was so overjoyed that the VC responded to my letter. I went ahead to read it. I won't attempt to quote exactly what he said. It's been a long time and my memory fails me when I try to recall exactly what he said, but among other things, he said something like, "I've taken notice of your concerns. My office is always open for discussion, and I hope we meet soon to have further deliberation on the issues raised."

I told Mawutor, "Guess what happened... the VC responded to my letter." She said, "You don't mean it." I responded, "I mean it." I showed her the letter and she said, "At long last, you'll be heard by someone who can actually do something about your situation."

I got a call on my phone one afternoon. The voice on the other side of the phone said, "This is the Personal Assistant of the VC. The VC wants to have a meeting with you, and I'm calling to schedule a time to meet him as soon as possible."

The day before the meeting with the VC, I remember going through my mind and jotting down all the things I would like to discuss with him. I didn't want to leave the meeting, go to the hall, and say, "Oh, I should have said this and that," or, "How come I didn't remember to tell him that?" I didn't want to leave any stone unturned, and I didn't want this one opportunity to slip without saying all the things I've been meaning to say. The day and time came, and I was ushered into the VC's office by the personal assistant. The VC welcomed me and I said, "Thank you." I remember his affable smile and how he tried to make me feel comfortable in his presence. We talked about the issues that surrounded my accommodation and how it later got resolved. We talked about how there could be a policy change so that, in the future, people with physical disabilities wouldn't face these challenges when admitted into the school. My challenges with access and how lecture venues were selected without consideration to the people with disabilities was also discussed thoroughly. Before the end of the discussion, I asked, "Is it possible for me to form a group of people with disabilities so that our views are expressed from one common voice?"

His response to all my concerns was positive. He said, "Every student on campus is my priority. Not some, but everyone, including people with disabilities. So we can work together to find ways and means to ensure safety for all." That response thawed my heart and made me happy for the future. I knew change wasn't going to be immediate, but I trusted that we could only make a difference if we began from somewhere—anywhere at all. I left the office of the VC very fulfilled and very hopeful, knowing that someone of his caliber was aware of my plight and was ready to work with me to make progress.

That wasn't the last meeting we had. We went on to have other meetings whenever he had the time. I remember in one of those meetings he asked me, "Are you part of the Hostel Committee of the SRC?" I responded, "No, I'm not." He said, "You should be part of such committees so you can use it as a channel to voice out the needs and wants of your group." I answered, "I'm not aware of the existence of such a committee and I don't know how to get involved."

It didn't take too long before I received a letter from the SRC (the Student Representative Council) inviting me to become a member of the Hostel Committee. At the time, the SRC of the UCC was putting up the biggest hostel on campus, so this committee was set up to ensure proper work was done on the project. I accepted their invitation and started attending their meetings. My main concern with the project was how to make it more accessible than the other hostel facilities on campus. So, at each meeting, I kept hammering the need for ramps connecting the floors of the building instead of only staircases. I also mentioned the sizes of the doors to the washrooms. I told them, "My scooter can't go through the washroom door. I must park it behind and use crutches or sometimes crawl inside the washroom. That must be changed in the new facility. A person using a wheelchair should be able to go through all the way to the washroom."

That hostel facility wasn't completed when I left the school in 2006. In 2010, when I visited the campus, I went to see the completed project and I was very proud of what I saw. I saw ramps connecting some of the floors (though not throughout) and it felt like a breath of fresh air. I went to visit the washroom and guess what? I could drive my wheelchair through the door. I wouldn't say they did those things because I mentioned them. Maybe they already had the idea of incorporating those functions or someone else, a professional, ensured it but it doesn't also take away the fact that I mentioned those things during our meetings.

I was going around campus trying to bring together all the people with disabilities so we could form a uniform voice as the VC advised, but some things never changed, especially my struggle with climbing long stairs before going to class. I was still relying on friends and other kind mates to carry me up the stairs to the lecture hall. I still tried, mostly unsuccessfully, to get lecture halls swapped so the lectures I was attending would be on the ground floor. Nothing changed in that direction, and I had to go through the occasional fall before getting up there for lectures. Some found it funny. Some looked me in the face and told me, "We can't swap a whole class just because of one person. Climbing is an exercise. It won't kill you."

"What doesn't kill you makes you stronger," they said, but in my case, what didn't kill me made me weaker. Climbing didn't kill me, but one day, it nearly did. I was on my way up to write a final year exam. The exam hall was on the third floor of the science rooftop. I remember that day and getting ready to go to the hall and write the exam. It had always been my character to be at the exam hall at least thirty minutes beforehand. It gave me the opportunity to relax, reflect, and put myself together before the exams started. The exam was at 3:00 pm, so exactly at 2:20 pm, I started my scooter. It didn't respond. I tried several times to put the ignition on, but it didn't respond. *Maybe it wasn't well charged. Let me put it on charge for a while,* I said to myself.

After a while, I tried to turn on the ignition and again, it didn't respond. I employed all the troubleshooting tricks I knew about the scooter, and it still didn't respond. I was running late, so I decided to use the crutches and walk. Mawutor was already gone, so I had to walk all alone to the exam hall. When I got to the staircase, there was no one around to help and I couldn't wait because I didn't know how long it was going to be before someone came by. Time was of the essence here, so one after the other, I moved my legs clumsily over each stair. Soon

I was on the first floor. "Two more floors to go," I said in my head. I was already sweating and panting but I had no option but to continue going. In the middle of the second staircase of the second floor, my left caliper broke. I started losing balance, so I tried leaning on my left clutches to maintain my balance. Little did I know that the left clutch was also not well positioned, so it crumpled under my weight and I fell down.

I started rolling down the stairs, somersaulting along the way, until I landed on the landing of the staircase. I'd fallen many times on staircases and many times, I got up, dusted myself off, and began again. At some point, I felt and believed that falling on stairs was part of the package of being physically disabled. Everyone thought it was normal. Those who could make a change didn't because they felt that it was normal. That day, when I got up from the landing, I realized something had changed. I tried standing on my right leg but the pain I felt brought me down immediately. That was when I realized the kneecap of my right leg had been dislocated. I started screaming in pain and that got people rushing to my aid. They saw me on the floor and asked, "What is wrong? What happened to you?" I told them, "I just fell from the top there and my other leg—the strong one—is also broken."

They didn't know what to do and I didn't know either. I started making phone calls to my friends but at that time the exam was in session so none of them responded to my calls. Then I remembered one of our professors, Prof Awusabo Asare, who helped me once upon a time when my scooter got stuck. I called his number, and he sent his driver for me. I still didn't know where to go from where I was lying; whether to be carried to my room, the examination hall, or to the hospital, and if hospital, then which hospital? I made a call to Brother Tarcicious, the founder of Nsawam Orthopedic Center. I told him what had happened to my knee and he said, "We can't do anything about it here since it's your knee, so the best place to go is St. Joseph's Hospital in Koforidua."

That day, those around me bundled me up into Prof. Awusabo's car and I was taken to Koforidua and St. Joseph's Hospital. My knee was heavily swollen and the pain was so unbearable that I wanted them to do something immediately to help heal my knee but the doctor said, "Your knee is dislocated and you'll need to go through therapy to slowly heal. It's unfortunate we don't have a knee specialist in Ghana to have a look at it and even if there was a specialist, it would be very difficult to restore your knee to become just as it was before the accident." So, from that day, I knew I wouldn't leave the facility looking the way I used to.

After two days at St. Joseph I was very calm and in a good state of mind, so the school authorities brought the exam I missed to me at the hospital and I wrote it there. Afterward, I started going through a series of therapy. After a few weeks, the pain subsided, but I couldn't stand on the affected leg. The doctor said, "It will be very hard for you to rest all your weight on that leg. It's not as strong as it used to be, and it has to be given some support." I remember measurements were taken of my legs and sent to Nsawam OTC for new calipers to be made for both of my legs. That was when I realized the more I climb the educational ladder, the more complex my disability becomes. But the good thing that happened to me in this journey was that I started believing strongly in Isaiah 43:2: "When you pass through the waters, I will be with you; and when you pass through the rivers, they will not sweep over you. When you walk through the fire, you will not be burned; the flames will not set you ablaze." And that keeps me going even today as I narrate these events in my life. I still feel that burning sensation that there is a supernatural power watching over me despite all odds.

Mom was with me through it all. My husband was too, now a tutor at Gbewaa training college in Pusiga in the Upper East Region of Ghana. He was very far away from Koforidua so he couldn't come immediately when the accident happened, but later he came and stayed for a while. Since my mother was around, he went back to Pusiga and visited me whenever he was able to. This was one of the more challenging moments of my life—to realize that I had lost the one leg that had supported me through it all. After spending about a month at St. Joseph, I became a little bit stronger, so I went back to campus to write the remaining papers, after which I returned to St. Joseph to continue with my therapy.

All the struggles, pain, and drama made my graduation day a very special day for me.

This was because I had grown to strongly believe in what scripture says in 1 Corinthians 10:13: "No temptation has overtaken you except what is common to mankind. And God is faithful; He will not let you be tempted beyond what you can bear. But when you are tempted, he will also provide a way out so that you can endure it." Mom was there and my husband was there. A few family members also came around to witness that day. The pride in my mother's eyes said it all. I didn't know what she thought about when she saw me in my gown and cap, but I could imagine her thinking of where everything had started and thanking God for how far He had brought her daughter. At the graduation ceremony that day when my name was mentioned, I got up on my crutches and began walking to the stage for my award. The whole gathering got up on their feet and gave me a standing ovation. All the falls, the breaking down, the disappointments, and the stress came down to that very moment, and I was very proud of myself for not giving up—for keeping on until the end.

CHAPTER 10 QUESTIONS:

−Considering this chapter's range of first-person, academic, and policy narratives, analyze the intersections between personal, historical, educational, social, and cultural responses to disability.

−How do you think we can normalize disability in a world where ableism has been the norm?

−How do these responses normalize expectations for people to adapt rather than systems changed?

−Do you think if we learn about disability from kindergarten, our policies will be so discriminatory like we have today?

Chapter 11
Egmont Højskloen

My degree program at the UCC ended and I returned to Nsawam. Before I returned, I had decided not to go back to the classroom because of my situation. Four years earlier, when I was teaching in Osae Djan, I had my right leg to stand on. It was the reason why I could stand in front of the class and teach. I came back to Nsawam with that right leg in calipers. My love for teaching the kids and helping them pass their final exams was still intact. Alas, I had no leg to stand on, to move around the class, mingle with them, and teach as I used to, so I opted to be placed in the District Education office instead.

It was the year 2006 and Mrs. Beatrice Lokko was the district director of education. She was very helpful to me. I wanted to be placed in the office but there was no vacant position for me to occupy. Mrs. Lokko said to me, "I'm going to keep you here as my personal assistant for the meantime as we ponder where we can permanently place you." So for a while I was the Personal Assistant to Mrs. Lokko, booking appointments, scheduling her meetings, and also scheduling her trips. The job was basically about knowing her schedules and planning them in such a way that there wouldn't be a conflict of events in her schedules.

As a personal assistant, I didn't have so much to do. I went to work in the morning and a few hours later, my job for the day was done. On days when the director traveled, I wouldn't have anything to do other than sit idly and engage in fruitless talk with other colleagues. It wasn't in my nature to waste time doing nothing so whenever the circuit supervisors were going to a School Performance Appraisal Meeting, I joined them. At all the places we traveled within the circuit, I used the opportunity to introduce myself to the school population and told them, "If you know someone with a physical disability like me who isn't going to school or being mistreated because of their condition, kindly tell them that someone wants to meet them. Let them know someone wants to give them a hand out of their struggle."

Almost all the time, I had kids walk up to me and tell me, "Madam, I know someone like that." Or "I know someone with your condition who had been cast away." I would tell them, "When you go home, ask them or their parents to come and see me at the education office." And they came. A lot of them came around, some with their parents and some with their dreams. They had dreams of going to school so they can have a better shot at life just like their able friends.

It was just around the same time that Mrs. Lokko called me and said to me, "For some time now you and I have been thinking of the right position in which to place you. Now I have an idea. That building there has been vacant for a very long time. We could use it as a resource center where you can train French teachers and other teachers who might need the training you could offer." I responded, "That's a great idea. We can have a resource center that caters to the needs of diverse people." I went into the building that day and assessed the work I had to do to put the building in shape to befit a resource center. It was an empty building that needed a facelift, but the District Education Office didn't have the budget to cover the expenses, so I had to find creative ways to raise money.

With the approval of Mrs. Lokko, I started writing letters to organizations and churches within the district to come to our aid. In my mind, the Center wasn't only going to be used for the training of French teachers. I had the whole community in mind, particularly the disabled community, to access education and vocational training and to also know their human rights. I can remember the immense contribution La Gray Pharmaceutical Factory made in the refurbishment of the place. I sent letters to churches and when I could, I went to the churches and spoke to them about the project and told them why they needed to contribute. Many churches came on board, donating many different items needed by the facility. Not too long afterward, the Resource Center became fully furnished and ready for use. From that point on, my position changed from Personal Assistant to Resource Center Coordinator.

I was coordinating French programs, providing special education training, and inviting resource providers to give special training to students and other people who needed it. I also used the center to cater for the needs of people with disabilities who were not in school. To sensitize the community and create awareness of the existence of the center, I moved from one church to another, telling them how people with disabilities could reach my office for assistance. I was often on the radio, Fawe FM in Nsawam, to speak on education for people with disabilities and the ways through which authorities can provide access to a person with a disability.

Through this and many other outreach programs, I became very well-known in the district. I became the unofficial voice and poster girl for people with disabilities. One morning, while in the office, a group of people came to see me. Their leader introduced himself as Wofa but I later got to know his full name as Francis Adu. He said, "We are witnesses to the good work you're doing for the people with disabilities in this community. That's why we've come to see you this morning. We are members of the Ghana Society of Physically Disabled (GSPD) and we are here today to ask you to become a member of the society so we can combine our efforts for the betterment of people with disabilities." I asked questions about their organizational structure in the district, what they've done so far, and what they intend to do to help people with disabilities.

Their goals appealed to me greatly, so I accepted their invitation. The next project we embarked on was to ensure that more members became aware of the Disability Common Fund from the government and how they could access such funds. It was during that project that the group decided to make me their president so I could become their mouthpiece. From the little investigation that we did, it came to our notice that the assembly managing the fund did not disburse the fund as instructed by the government. The leadership of GSPD booked a meeting with the then Municipal Chief Executive, Lawyer Nyarko Aidoo, and at the meeting, I asked him, "How is the Disability Common Fund for the district disbursed and who are the beneficiaries? Because none of our members have benefitted from the fund." He looked at me. Maybe he didn't think a time would come that someone would approach him with such a question. He answered, "That money is used for something else since no one has come forward to claim it. I've been using it to settle chieftaincy issues around here."

I was so angry that I didn't know what to say or do. This was a huge amount that could have brought some sort of comfort or relief to the people with disabilities, but our leader, a municipal executive, thought the best way to put that money to use was to use it to settle chieftaincy litigations. I made it clear to him that the community of people with disabilities was ready to access the fund, so kindly make it accessible as soon as possible or I would have no option but to escalate the issue to national level. His response didn't make it sound like he was ready to disburse the money to the disabled community. The next time I had the opportunity to speak on FAWE FM, I told the people exactly what our MCE was using their money for and how far we were ready to go to retrieve that amount. Maybe he heard what I said and wasn't pleased, because from then on, he avoided meetings with us. We went to his office on several occasions and he wasn't around. Even when we had booked appointments with him, he found an excuse not to be present.

The next available option was to report the issue to the GSPD National Executive. I remember talking to Alex Tetteh, the GSPD National Administrator at the time. He gave me a letter to send to the MCE. Among other things, the letter stated clearly that he should disburse the money to the people or face appropriate sanctions. When I delivered the letter to the MCE, he got so angry and questioned why we would go that far with the issue. I had no answer for him, but I told myself, *If only you did the right thing, this matter would have been settled within, but you kept playing hide and seek with us.*

The next time we had a meeting with him, he agreed to disburse the money. He said, "Yes, the money is ready, but we can't give physical cash to individuals, so instead we are going to buy them some of the basic things they need." I told him, "That's a good idea but these people need different things. Different things because they are in different situations. Some are in school. They'll need their fees paid. Some are learning trade, they'll need trade items. Some want to learn a vocation. We can't put all these people in one bracket and buy them what we think they need." He said, "Okay, then we'll pay the fees for all those in school."

And he did pay the fees for some of the people. We waited to see when he was going to buy the items for those who needed it, but that never happened. When we called him out on it, he said, "After paying the fees, there was nothing left to buy the items for those people." That man didn't want to be transparent with us. It was always back and forth with him until new government came into power. But I realized that before the members of GSPD would be able to access that fund without fail, they needed training on the fund guidelines. We built a curriculum around the National Guideline for them and took them through all they needed to do to be able to access the fund easily. The resource center became our training center, and they came by every day, learning what they needed to do to access the fund themselves.

Things got easier when we had a new MCE. He was ready to work with us. I was called to the meetings of the assembly often so they could listen to our needs and what they could do to meet them. Through those engagements, many people with disabilities were sent to school. Those who wanted to own stores, were given the stores, and those who wanted to learn a vocation were also provided with the appropiate assistance for them to achieve their dreams. I was so glad to work easily without much tension from MCE Dr. Adu-Twum and Mr. Frank Amoako-Dompreh during their terms in office.

One afternoon, I received a call from Alex Tetteh. He said, "There is a Danish International Development Agency (DANIDA) sponsored program for people with disabilities, and your group has nominated you to represent them in that program." I asked, "Where's the program taking place and when is it taking place?" He answered, "Actually, it's a one-year training program happening in Denmark, and you've been selected because you fit all the criteria they are looking for in the candidate." "Wait, you mean Denmark as in abroad?" I asked with a tint of surprise in my voice. He answered, "What other Denmark do you know apart from that one?" I couldn't hold myself together. Me? Going to Denmark? As in, I'm going to sit in a plane and fly? I was so happy I didn't know what to do. Alex told me, "You can come to the office tomorrow to get all the details."

First thing the next morning I was in Alex's office. He directed me to meet a three-member committee to discuss the details of the package. I went to meet the committee and one of the panel members laid down the requirements of the program to me. He said, "It's a DANIDA project and they are looking for a woman who is disabled and has at least a Bachelor's Degree and is already doing something to help people with disabilities." After telling me all of the details, he asked, "Is it something you're interested in?" "I'm interested," I responded, "I wish I would even be going tomorrow."

The rest was all paperwork. The GSPD bought me the plane ticket. I then went to the Danish embassy for a series of interviews, all the while working with the GSPD to ensure smooth traveling arrangements. In January 2007, I was at the airport getting ready to board the plane to Denmark. The whole thing looked surreal. When the plane was up in the sky, I gave a huge sigh of relief and started dreaming of Denmark. I thought about all the wonderful pictures and videos I had seen of Denmark and said to myself, *Me too, I'm going to see all those beautiful things and I'll have a story to tell when I return.* Some part of me was ready for the adventure and another part was ready to accept the realities of what was happening in my life. I took time to reflect on my life, where it all began and how far I'd come. That girl from a little town in the Volta region called Tegbi is now standing at the door of greatness and knocking. I didn't know who was going to open that door but I believed that the mighty name of God would make everything beautiful in the end ("He hath made everything beautiful in his time: also he hath set the world in their heart, so that no man can find out the work that God maketh from the beginning to the end." Ecclesiastes 3:11 KJV). I looked at the faces of people in the plane and imagined their reasons for traveling. "Are they going to do business? Are they going to meet families? Are they rich people who are just going on a vacation?"

I couldn't believe my eyes when we finally touched down at the Copenhagen airport. I said, "Wow, so it's true. How could a single place have all this beauty? This is heaven." Everything looked new to me. New, because I hadn't seen it all before. The airport was very busy with people moving up and down looking for something or someone or going through checks. I stood there for a while, took a long breath in, and looked around to find who were waiting for me. I looked up and saw a placard bearing my name. I approached the one carrying the placard and said, "Here I am." She smiled and said, "Welcome to Denmark. I'll take you to your hotel."

It was at the hotel that I realized I wasn't the only one coming to Denmark to do the course. There were Nigerians, Kenyans, Ugandans, and other nationals who had all traveled from their countries to Denmark for the program. I looked at them and realized we all had one thing in common: disabilities. We were a rainbow of people with different forms of disabilities. All of us were kept in a hotel waiting for others who were yet to reach Denmark. On the third day, we were all bused to Egmont Højskolen in Hov to begin our training.

On the bus to Hov, we interacted with each other to get to know each other and build friendships. That was when I met Irene Nabalamba, a Ugandan who was also disabled in the leg—the right leg. We got along and later became next door neighbors on campus. It was Irene who came to knock on my door one day and said, "Sefakor, they say we are going to swim and we have to be in our swimsuit. Can you imagine how our little legs would be in a swimsuit?" I responded, "Oh you've also been thinking about that? It's been my headache since I heard about the swimming. I'm not comfortable at all going to expose my little leg out there."

So that day, we wore our swimsuits underneath our normal dresses and went to the pool. When the instructor Tina Arvid saw us, she was taken aback; "Are you guys not swimming?" We chorused, "Yes, we are here to swim." She looked at us from hair to toe, looking all surprised. She asked, "You are going to swim looking like that? In your normal clothes?"

One needs to understand our sensitivity towards our own bodies. We come from a place where being like us was not seen as normal, so you spent the rest of your life hiding who you are in clothes. Exposing that part of ourselves all of a sudden felt like we were naked in front of the world, exposing what we've been hiding since childhood. It felt awkward and embarrassing at the same time. So we would rather swim in covers than to expose our dangling little legs.

But as I was standing there and watching people with all forms of disabilities enter the pool, a sudden gush of confidence went through me—like a new blood seeping through my veins. There were people with all forms of disabilities in the pool. Some even entered the pool with their aiding machines. I told myself, *It's now or never, Sefakor. Get in there and enjoy the water. If none else, you'll end up learning a new skill— swimming.* I looked at Irene and she was getting ready to enter the pool. I also took off my normal clothes, wearing just the swimming suit, and entered the pool. It was still awkward, but I was determined to do it anyway. As time went on and we visited the pool on several occasions, I learned to live comfortably with the experience, and everything became normal.

Egmont Højskolen was all about learning through activities and observations. We observed how people with disabilities lived their lives in Denmark, thought about the impact, and thought how we could replicate the same in our own countries. At the end of the whole year course, we were tasked with an assignment to come up with a project to embark on when we went back to our countries. I thought about my advocacy project for people with disabilities and how I could come up with a project to improve the lives of the people I left behind.

I remembered one day when we visited a facility that left a very huge impression on my mind. It was a factory where bicycle rims were manufactured. All the people in the production line were people with mental health disabilities who had been trained to manufacture bicycle rims. They were positioned at different stages of the production line where they had been tasked to do just one thing. The task was very routine, and these people did it without any fault. That made me think about how people with cognitive disabilities were left to rot in my country. I said to myself, *If only this can be replicated in my country, we could drastically reduce the number of people roaming and idling in the street.*

We were always moving from one place to another, analyzing how disability was managed in different situations. I made it a point to start recording some of the areas we visited and how those there were excellently managing different kinds of people with different forms of disability. In my mind, I was building a video library that would help me showcase all the things I learned to other people and use it in drafting policy statements to support people with disabilities in Ghana.

The biggest thing Egmont taught me was how warped the lens was through which we perceived disability in Ghana and Africa as a whole. The day I came to Egmont and saw all the forms of disabilities people came with, some I didn't even know the name of. I looked at myself and said, "So what's my problem? Do I call what I have a disability?" I looked at my new friends and my disability paled. The most amazing part was that all these people had a job to do. They were not neglected; they were not left behind or cast to the street to beg for food to eat. Because of good policies put in place by the government of Denmark, all people had something to do, something that their disability would allow them to do without problems. I compared it to my country where someone with a goiter ran to the street and begged for food only because they could not find a place in the community where their abilities could be tapped. We were concentrating so much on people's disabilities that we missed their abilities.

Egmont taught me to look out for the abilities in the people we call disabled so when the one-year course was over, I knew exactly what I was going to do. When I was asked, I told them, "I'm going to use the media—every available media channel—to sensitize people and those in authority to the fact that there are many things people with disabilities can accomplish. If only we can identify the best ways to integrate them into the society, they too can contribute their quota to the development of the nation."

CHAPTER 11 QUESTIONS:

–Advocacy is aimed at changing government policies and it must have a strategy which is the road map that keeps you focused and guided. It needs to be time bound with the right message. An advocacy needs to have objectives which must be small enough to achieve something of value within a reasonable time. All these points need to be directed to a targeted audience who will make the social change you want to see in the society.

–Discuss based on this chapter.

Chapter 12
The Day I Died

My studies in Egmont ended in August 2007, but I spent some time in Denmark enjoying the place and learning about other things I didn't get the chance to learn for myself due to schooling. There were so many beautiful things to see and beautiful places to visit. There were relationships to be consolidated and bonds created between the many friends I met while there, so I used the months ahead to do all that until November 2007 when I packed bag and baggage and returned to Ghana. It was when I got to the Kotoka International Airport that I realized how much I'd missed home. The air that greeted me at the airport didn't feel like the air in Denmark, but it came with the warmth one can only feel at home. The voices and greetings gave me soothing assurance that indeed I had come back to a place where I belonged. It might not be as beautiful as the one I just left, but it had its own beauty which was mostly expressed in the faces of people you saw and how they were ever ready to embrace you and welcome you back home.

It was all joy when I got home. Seeing the familiar faces of those I left behind, especially those of Mom and my husband. Tasting the ever-delicious familiar meals from my mother and finally resting my back in my own bed brought a feeling of comfort I had not experienced in a while. People in Denmark (and I would later learn that this is true of people in America, too) eat a lot of bread (pizza, sandwiches, buns, etc.). I told myself, "This is home and I'm glad to be back." That night, we couldn't keep quiet—my mom, my siblings, my husband and I. They gathered around as I told them the stories of Denmark; how beautiful the place was, how people with disabilities were treated, and many other wonderful things I saw while there. I could sense the happiness in their voices when they spoke to me. It sounded like they were saying, "We are very happy to have you back."

The next Monday I reported to work at the Resource Center of the Education Service. That was another happy welcome back for me. The cheers, the tease, the many "Welcome from Denmark" greetings filled my heart with so much gratitude and filled my day with a little magic. It was like a victorious return of a soldier from war. All that and more made me determined to carry out the project I had brought back from Denmark. I wanted to make a change in the environment where the people with disabilities were and also create a platform where they could access information. I needed to better their lives.

I started on GTV—Ghana's premium television. When I got introduced to Marcus, a producer of the Morning Show of GTV, he asked me; "What do you seek to bring on board and what do you seek to achieve in the end?" My answer was simple; "I want to show Ghanaians, especially people of authority, that there's a place for the people with disabilities and that place is not on the street where they must beg. Through my videos and educational programs, they'll learn that people with disabilities deserve a chance and equal opportunities in order to shine."

Not too long afterwards I was given a slot on GTV to begin my advocacy project. That was when the video library I built while in Egmont became very useful. During my TV show, I would show clips about how disabled people lived their lives in other parts of the world. The videos were categorized to show different ways people with disabilities contributed to nation building. Some days I showed how people with disabilities could contribute in agriculture and other times I would show how they can contribute in various other industries. After the clip was an in-house discussion when we opened the telephone lines for people to call in and share their views concerning the video of the day.

During the call-in sessions our telephone lines often got jammed due to so many people trying to call in at the same time. They all wanted to share their views and some wanted to make suggestions. To me, that was a sign that the message was getting to people. One day, after the program, someone called in and asked, "I'm a PWD and I've been following your program. I want to say that I'm inspired to go out there and make a difference, but I want to know where to start—which government agency to speak to and how to get there." At another time, it was somebody who was encouraging us to do more than just sitting on TV. The opinions were diverse but the beauty of it all was that people were getting the message and were ready to do something for themselves and their communities. All they needed was education and a little push, which I was always there to provide.

I was in Ghana, but I continued maintaining relationships with the people I met in Denmark. One of those people was Karen. I spoke to her daily and, at one point, pitched a training idea to her. I told her, "I have a group of people here who could benefit from your expertise. Do you mind coming over to Ghana to train them?" She responded with cheer in her voice, "No, I don't mind. In fact, I would be very happy to come over and do that." A month or so after this conversation, Karen came to Ghana.

She taught our members how to make a simple greeting card. All we needed to learn and create these cards were papers—used papers. So I went around some institutions including GES, La Gray, and printing press offices collecting used papers for the training. We soaked these papers in water over night and pounded them in mortar. We designed them differently with different wood-carved designs. This was followed by drying according to size and the colors we used. In the end, we would have paper cards that we designed into beautiful greeting cards. Our members were very happy about the training, and they were deeply involved from start to the end. Some ended up creating beautiful cards that were sold and money generated from it.

The amazing thing was, after the training, Karen bought all the cards that the trainees were able to produce and sent them to Denmark where she was able to sell them as souvenirs. This papermaking enterprise became an avenue from which the members of the GSPD could raise money to cater for themselves. Some did and others stopped along the way. When asked why they stopped, they said, "It's not easy to get papers—a lot of papers—to produce the cards. In actuality, the problem wasn't about finding papers. It was about commitment and zeal. If they wanted to find papers, they could have. Instead, they relaxed and gave up because it wasn't easy to get used papers. Nothing good comes easy, they say, but these people wanted an easy way to get good things.

My TV program continued rolling. Apart from that, I moved from one radio station to another advocating for the rights of people with disabilities and educating authorities on why our public institutions such as schools and hospitals should be made accessible to the PWD communities. Getting access to people in authority was easier when I became a member of the National Advocacy team of the then Ghana Federation of the Disabled, which is now the Ghana Federation of Disability Organizations (GFD). Through that, I got the chance to go to the parliament of Ghana, lobby the committees for disability laws, and debate policies concerning disabilities. I could sense the impact of our outreach and that gave us the strength to go the extra mile to ensure laws were enacted and policies were put in place to support people with disabilities.

In 2008, at the height of my advocacy project, I became pregnant. I thought nothing could stop me from doing the work that I loved so much, but that year of 2008, all it took for me to lay down my advocacy tools was a pregnancy. A pregnancy that nearly took my life and the life of my babies away.

◊

I got pregnant in February. Per the permutations of my husband and I, I was going to deliver in November, the month my husband and I were born in. After the first trimester, I realized my feet were getting swollen and my fingers, too. We thought it was normal. I'd seen a lot of pregnant women with swollen feet and noses, and they were fine. In the fourth month, I remember we went to see my doctor, Dr. Ablorh, who was taking care of me in the Nsawam hospital. After the scan that day he told me, "It looks like you're carrying twins. That's how it looks, but I can't confirm until your next visit." He did not know he was confirming my secret prayers all these years because I had always prayed for twins (a girl and a boy). All I wanted was to suffer once and have two results.

Bearing twins has a way of making the heart happy. If you come from this side of the world where bearing twins is considered as a special blessing, then you understand my joy when the doctor gave me the news. I prayed for it to be true and hoped that God would answer my prayers, but the month ahead became very difficult for me. I had pains all over my body and experienced vertigo whenever I was on elevated surfaces. Even sitting on my bed gave me vertigo. At one point I remembered the swollen feet and the pains got so intense that I couldn't sit. Mom laid a mattress on the floor for me and that was where I slept. I was bedridden for the rest of my pregnancy period. There were two nurses who came around alternatively to check on me. They'd check my BP and tell me, "Your BP is too high for a pregnant woman." It never went down. It was either up or the same as when they checked the last time.

That state of helplessness when my mother bathed me and cleaned me up brought back memories of the days when I was young. It was difficult for me to see my mom go through all that again, but I couldn't wish my situation away. I only had to bear it until the babies were delivered. One afternoon, I remembered feeling very hungry, so I called out to my mom to prepare amadetsi and amorkple for me, which she brought in no time. I sat on the bed and ate the food. Mom came for the plate and gave me water to wash my hands. The last memory I had of that moment was putting my hand in the water. I didn't remember anything that happened afterward.

According to my mother's narration of events, she saw me washing my hand in the bowl when suddenly I flipped backwards and fell to the ground. I began shaking violently on the ground—something that looked like I was having a fit with the pregnancy, which is called eclampsia in medical terms. Since my husband wasn't around, my mom said she screamed out for help and some people, like my next-door neighbors called Uncle Francis, Nana, Uncle Charles, and Attamami, came in to help rush me to the Nsawam hospital. My pregnancy was seven months along, and my stomach looked bulgier than a normal seven-months stomach. I was in a coma when they got to the hospital. I wasn't moving and my breath was getting thinner and thinner. At the hospital, we were received by Doctor Abloh, who did some checks on me and said something like, "She's carrying twins, and looking at her condition, we ought to perform an emergency cesarean section to remove the babies. Currently, we don't have incubators here to house the babies, so the best thing is to refer her to Korle-Bu teaching hospital."

It was a Wednesday evening and we got to Korle-Bu a little bit late, so they couldn't perform the C-section until Thursday morning. I was still in a coma when the babies were removed from my tummy—a boy and a girl. The expectation was that I would awaken after the C-section, but I didn't. On Friday, I was still in a coma. That was when they declared me dead. According to my mother, a nurse walked up to her and told her, "Your daughter couldn't make it so we are processing her for the mortuary." My mom abruptly started crying. She informed other family members who were around, and they all began wailing. My mom told my husband, "We've lost her but the kids are alive so we should start looking for a nursing mother to take care of them for when they come out of the incubator."

My husband called his sisters to inform them and ask them to be ready to take care of the babies. My mom kept going in and out of the maternity ward to ensure that the preparation went smoothly. When it was time to take me to the mortuary, they got information from the mortuary man that the mortuary was full, so they had to keep me in the waiting room until Saturday morning when families of the dead would come around to remove some of the dead bodies for burial.

For the whole night on Friday, I was dressed up and kept in the waiting room to be transferred to the mortuary on Saturday morning. According to the nurse on duty that night, I started coughing somewhere in the middle of the dawn. He wanted to be sure he was hearing right, so he opened the door, came to stand next to my body, and watched. He said, "Not too long afterward, she coughed again and again and again. That was when I realized that she wasn't dead after all."

On Saturday morning, when my mother and my husband got to Korle-Bu, the nurses on duty gave them the news; "In the middle of the dawn she coughed and we realized she wasn't dead, so we have moved her back to the maternity ward." My mom was like, "Who said there is no God? He is a miracle worker!" The nurse led them to the maternity ward to have a look at me. I was in an oxygen mask and was looking better than before. They had made plans for my absence and given roles to various family members to perform in my absence. Now, the situation had changed. I was alive. It had to be the hand of God that pulled me out of the dungeon of the dead because there was so much I had to do. Those feeble babies he gave me needed me, so the Lord gave me a second chance to complete his will. Oh, how I wished I had seen heaven!

You can imagine the glow in my mother's eyes when she found me alive. The gush of happiness that rushed through the vein of my husband when he learned his sweetheart was still around. All plans had to revert to default because I was alive—once more. They say that a day or two later I came fully back to life and started talking and asking questions.

I asked about my babies and how long I'd been in the hospital. "The babies are doing well," they said, "and we are grateful to God that you're here with us."

The first time I set my eyes on the babies, I nearly shed tears of happiness. Knowing they were still alive regardless of everything we'd been through got to me emotionally. I looked at them and how tiny they looked—my heart was filled with nothing but gratitude. The two months that they were kept in the incubator were some of the toughest moments of my life. I couldn't breastfeed my kids because I had no milk and the nurses were not allowing the babies to be fed with processed foods. It broke my heart somedays but there was nothing I could do because I could not get enough breast milk when I expressed the milk for them. Some days I would look at their faces and be filled with disappointment for what we were going through, and some days I would look at their faces and say, "Don't worry little kids, we will pull through eventually. We will make it in the end even though it's hard today."

Two months after, they were declared stable and we were discharged from Korle-Bu hospital. When we got home, we tried as hard as we could to hide the babies from strangers because they were so tiny and not easy on the eyes. I remember one day my younger sister Selorm walked up to me and asked, "Are you sure these are normal human beings because we can only see their heads." She wasn't telling a lie and her concern was valid. We all knew how babies looked but these babies were not looking like the normal babies we've come to know: big heads and tiny bodies.

In the mornings I'd wrap them up on my chest and sit in the morning sun with them. According to the doctors, they needed this to gain the necessary vitamins for their growth. For a whole year we went through this process with them. Sometimes my mother would do it or my siblings would do it. I couldn't go to work and I couldn't do all the advocacy work I used to do because I needed to be with these kids every day.

Eleven months after their birth, they had grown beautifully and had grown to a level where we could expose them to friends and other colleagues who cared to come look at them. Around the same time, I regained my strength and shed off all pains and postpartum depression. I told my husband, "The kids are now looking better. I think we can now outdoor them and do their dedication in church." He agreed with me that it was about time we did their dedication, so we made arrangements with the church and one Sunday, the whole family went in a celebratory mood to dedicate the children to the Lord. The pastor asked; "What name are you giving to them?"

Months before that day, I was reading Psalm 92:10-11 when God planted their names in my heart through the verses. I told my husband about it and in the end, we were able to make a name in our language out of the verses. So when the pastor asked about their names that day, I said, "The boy is Edonusem, meaning 'my God has strengthened me.' The girl is Edomdedzi, meaning 'my God has exalted me like a wild ox.'" He anointed them and said a prayer, committing them into the hands of the Lord. This is why their names are so unique and never given to anyone on this earth before.

CHAPTER 12 QUESTIONS:

- What are the things that resonate with you or trigger some thought in you in this chapter?

- From this narration, what do you think are the challenges we have in the health system?

- Imagine the trouble my family went through when I was declared death and find some solutions.

Chapter 13
The U.S.A.

Early in 2010, I was on the GTV Breakfast Show doing my advocacy when someone called the TV station and left his number. He said, "Kindly tell her to call me after the program." When I finished the program and the number was given to me, I was sort of surprised and asked myself, *Who could this person be?* I would only know if I called him, so I picked up my phone and dialed the number. A voice said, "Hello, who am I speaking with?" It was a male's voice. I told him, "I'm Sefakor. You left your number with GTV and said that I should give you a call." He responded, "Yeah, I did. I hope you're doing good." I answered, "I'm doing very well but who am I talking to?" You could sense a smile in his voice when he said, "There's no need to know who I am. There's feedback I would like to give to you. I've followed your work both on television and on the radio. I think you're doing amazing work. I also think that you're a bit aggressive with the way you make your case. You can slow down, make your submissions patiently, and focus a little bit more on policy gaps and functional practices. That would go a long way to help the success of your work."

The fact that I didn't know who I was talking to made me a little bit anxious, but I was grateful for the kind of feedback he gave me, so I said, "Thank you so much for your thoughts. I'll consider them and polish my act." He then asked, "Would you like to further your education in advocacy so you can, in the future, do full-time advocacy work?" I responded, "Yes, that's exactly what I want to do in the near future." He went on to tell me about many educational scholarship opportunities I could look into if I was interested. He then told me, "There's one scholarship I would recommend to you. It is an International Fellowship Program, look at it. If you apply and get selected, it would help your cause greatly."

Few moments later, he sent me the link on my phone. He didn't want to meet me, and he didn't want to reveal himself to me. To this date, I don't know who that person was. He said, "I'm glad you would like to go to school and I'm glad I could help you in any way that I can. What's important now is for you to get more education so you can use your pain and grievances more positively toward policy-making and practices rather than just broadcasting the narratives."

I went online and checked the link he sent. It was the International Ford Foundation Scholarship application. When I checked the deadline, it had only twenty-four hours before it expired. I told myself, "This is it. By any means I have to finish applying for this scholarship before the deadline." I was racing against time, but I was careful not to make any mistake that would cause my application to be rejected. I finished just in time and submitted my application. The only thing left for me to do was to put my references together and submit, but the scholarship schedule permitted us to submit references on a later date, so that didn't become a major problem for me.

After submission, I had to wait and pray for a call. The waiting period is always the difficult part when you want something so desperately. I checked my emails every now and then, hoping I'd receive the notice that I'd been picked. Each passing day came with nothing, but I kept hope alive knowing that I did everything right in the submission of the application. Three or so months later, I received a message from the Foundation. I should have been excited upon sighting the email, but I was cautious not to jubilate prematurely. *What if they're telling me my application didn't qualify? Let me read the content first,* I said to myself.

I read through the content of the email and found that it was an invitation by the scholarship committee for an interview at African Regent Hotel, Airport Accra. Saying I was excited would be an understatement. I couldn't hold myself together. I called my mom and gave her the news. She was equally happy for me. She said, "Congratulations; you'll ace the interview. I trust you." On the morning of the interview, I said a silent prayer: *God, you know I need this more than ever. Kindly see me through.* When I got to the African Regent Hotel, the number of people there was more than I anticipated; *All these people are attending the interview? What's the probability that I'm going to be picked, anyway?* For the first time in a very long while, I began to question my capability. Everything I saw that day was intimidating. Too many people vying for too few spots and every person I met looked very prepared and ready to win. I was ushered into a room to meet the interview panel of four black people and eight white people. Seeing the seriousness on their faces, I started shivering. I questioned my worth and again, I questioned my abilities. The voices in my head all of the sudden started giving me all the reasons why I couldn't qualify. *See their faces. Are you sure you can answer their questions? Eight of them are white; how are you going to communicate in a way that they can understand you? Are you sure when they speak in their accent you will be able to grasp what they're saying? Just turn around and go home; you can't play at this level.* Before the panel could utter a word to me, I took a deep breath and shut up the voices in my head. They said hello and I said hello back, feeling diminished in their presence. They started asking about my advocacy work and the various things I'd done to help the community of the disabled. They asked about changes I'd brought to the lives of those I'd fought for and the numerous projects I'd embarked on to bring changes in the lives of the disabled community.

I'd spent all of my adult life in the field of advocacy work, so the answers to such questions came easily to me. But as the interview progressed, I was pushed to the limits of my wits to bring out answers to questions I never thought I would be asked in an interview. Through it all, I managed to stay calm, stick to the topic, and speak honestly on the issues raised. First interview over. I had to wait and see whether or not I was going to be selected. The tough period is always the waiting period, but after three months, I received an email to attend a second interview, which I did and was successful. I was called again to attend a third interview. That was the hardest one, and my character really was tested. I wanted the scholarship more than anything, so I always went prepared. The numbers kept dropping at each level. People you met and became friends with were dropped. It broke their hearts and it scared you. You asked yourself, *Who's next? Am I the next person to be dropped?*

After the third interview, I got the call that I'd been selected. Over two hundred people showed up for the interviews but only twenty of were selected. I should have been happy. I should have thrown myself on the floor and jubilated, but I couldn't. Being selected wasn't the end of the story. There was TOEFL to write, there was GRE to write, and I had to pass these two exams before I could finally call myself a Ford Fellow. And these two examinations more or less determined the kind of school you would be admitted to. All the selected candidates were enrolled at Ghana Institute of Managment and Public Administration (GIMPA) to study these courses, write the exam, and pass before we could be assigned to schools abroad. All the while I was still working at the Ghana Education Service (GES). Combining the training with GES work and motherhood wasn't an easy thing to do, but thank God for family—my mom, my husband, and other distant family who were there for me. I was able to go through the training successfully and came out with flying colors. When I finally got the news that I had passed the TOEFL and GRE courses, I said a prayer in my heart; "Thank you God for making this possible." I had a little jubilation with the family and moved on to the most important things like how my twins were going to be taken care of while I was away.

Mom always came to the rescue. She was there when these kids were born, and she was a major helping hand in bringing them up when I had to leave them. She had to come back to Nsawam to help my husband take care of the kids. Edonusem and Edomdedzi were two years and some months old when I finally left the shores of Ghana to go to the United States and begin my master's program as a Ford Fellow in World Learning-Graduate School for International Training (SIT) in Brattleboro, Vermont.

I was faced with accessibility challenges on my first day at the SIT campus. Before my arrival, the school authorities knew I was a person with a disability but they didn't know the extent of my disability. Or if they knew, then they might have underestimated the height of my disability. They might have thought that my kind of disability was normal and as such could use the facilities all the people used. So, when it came to accommodation, they placed me on the top floor of a storied building where I needed to use a lift to access my room. On the very first day that I tried to use the lift, it didn't work. I stayed in the lift for a while and pressed all the buttons that ought to be pressed, but this lift never went up. One of the school authorities told me, "Sorry about the failure. This lift hadn't been in used for so many years because we haven't had a person with a disability in a long while, but don't worry, we'll make a place for you downstairs so you won't need to use the lift."

There was a classroom downstairs that was attached to the multi-cultural department. This classroom had a washroom and other facilities that could make living there easy. Two or three days later, the school authorities repartitioned the classroom and turned it into a beautiful bedroom with everything that I would need to make living there easier for me. I was surprised at the kind of work they had to do to make it possible to move me there. I started recalling my experience at the University of Cape College (UCC) and how difficult it was for the authorities there to make a change just to accommodate me. At SIT, the change was quick and was done without any confrontations whatsoever. That was my first culture shock when I got to SIT. The authorities kept apologizing to me for the inconvenience: "We are so sorry about the situation, and we hope to work together to make your stay comfortable."

From that day onwards, I started comparing my experiences at UCC and SIT. All the troubles I went through at UCC could have been averted if authorities saw the need to do it. They were not ready to change anything because of just one person. They were like, "It's only you so why do we have to go through all that struggle to make a change just because of you?" That was why I continued attending classes on top floors and kept falling down staircases. No one cared to make a change. At SIT, they immediately saw my situation and started making changes to accommodate me. All the classes I had to use the lift to attend were brought downstairs. And the good thing was, I didn't need to chase anyone around making complaints here and there. They knew the extent of my disability and didn't want their environment to be an obstacle to my living there, so they made changes in venues to make it easier for me to attend all the lectures. That was something I was always grateful for. It doesn't mean I didn't face physical impediment. I did.

One of the major access challenges I had to deal with throughout my two years stay on the SIT campus was how to access the school's main auditorium. The auditorium was built up on a hill and could only be accessed by a flight of stairs. That brought back memories of my days in MOMACO, where I had to climb many stairs to get to the school's main block. At SIT, I never even thought for a day to try to climb the stairs leading to the main auditorium. If I did and I fell, that would have been the end of me, so I couldn't attend all of the major programs the school organized at the main auditorium. Unlike other portions of the campus they could retrofit to make it more accessible, the school's main auditorium was inadaptable. It was an old building with old fashioned accessories that made it difficult to retrofit. So one day during a school discussion on inclusion, I asked my friends, "Do you guys believe for a second that someone like me can claim inclusion on this campus? Look at my situation and the nature of accessibility on this campus and judge for yourselves." They were quiet for a while, thinking about the question I'd just asked. Then, all of the sudden, a conversation broke out on campus about the topic. There were professors I visited and spoke to. Each time I had the opportunity, I brought up the issue of inclusion and accessibility. One professor, Jeff Unsicker, once told me, "If you continue talking about it without doing anything, the problem won't get solved. You're a policy student. If you team up with mates, do research, and write a policy brief about the issue, the school authorities will do something about it."

I took his advice and teamed up with two friends, Nick Cream and Dianna Haines. As I learned in my policy analysis and advocacy class, forming alliances is very important for policy change. In view of this, the three of us conducted campus research to ascertain whether or not the campus was accessible enough. In the process, the three of us went around interviewing students, teachers, and non-teaching staff to seek their views on the subject. In the end, our research findings were very clear; the school campus was not accessible enough. Most people pointed out the hilly nature of the campus and how difficult it was for people with physical disabilities to function without barriers. Others talked about limited accessories to help people with disabilities to function. Most of the views surveyed confirmed that the school needed to do more if they wanted to ensure inclusion.

When we presented our research as a school project, each of us was given an A. That was confirmation of our hard work and dedication to a cause, but I didn't want it to end there. I didn't want the project to be just a school project, so I spoke to my team members; "Team, this is a very good project and we don't have to let it end on the shelves of the school. From what I know, if we push it a little bit, the school will take notice and start to implement our findings." Nick agreed and was ready to go the length with me to push our research to the school's authority. Dianna was hesitant. From what I got from her posture; she wasn't sure that it was a good thing for an African student to question an American school system. She found it risky, so she backed off. That didn't stop me and Nick from pursuing our agenda.

I sent an email to our school's president requesting an audience for the two of us. Not long afterward, he accepted the invitation. That day, I went with Nick and a copy of our research. The school president welcomed us and said, "Now tell me, what's the discussion about?" I started talking about our research—what made us start doing the research, the processes we went through to achieve our aim, and how we arrived at our conclusions. Judging by the glow in his eyes as I spoke, I realized he was very interested in our subject. He kept nodding all throughout and listened attentively as we spoke. In the end he said, "Impressive. I'm really glad you guys were able to bring this up. This campus has been here for so many years and many people with different disabilities have passed through the corridors of this school but no one complained or did anything of this nature so it was easy for us to think everything was well. Thank you so much for bringing this up and I can assure you something will be done about it."

Some days after our meeting, I got an email from the school's board inviting me to attend their meeting. I did, and from then on, it became the norm. At each meeting I attended they sought my input on certain changes they wanted to bring on the campus. They wanted to know how beneficial those changes would be to me and other physically disabled people in society. We deliberated things they could do to ensure total inclusion on campus. This series of meetings went on for a long time until one day they told me, "We are writing to the federal government to seek grants in order to retrofit some areas of the campus that can be changed." That was great news, but the next question was, "Is the federal government going to approve the grants?" One day at a meeting the chair announced, "Our grant requests have been approved by the federal government. We should soon expect resources from the government and begin work on some areas of the campus."

I was a witness to the various changes they made around campus to ensure its accessibility for all. Ramps were introduced at places that needed them. Lifts were also changed in some facilities on the campus. I looked around and saw all the various changes going on and I couldn't be prouder of what we did. It all began as research work but we didn't let it end there. We needed to see change so we worked at it and in the end, the results became visible for all to see. To me, it was a victory for advocacy. And there was one thing I learned: we don't have to remain quiet on things that threaten our communal safety as people. If we keep quiet, nothing will change, and we will continue to suffer. It is when we decide to engage those in authority that we begin to see changes. And in the process of seeking to change things, we had to ensure that we talked to the right people—people who are in the position to affect the kind of changes you want to see.

This victory made me realize that there were so many other things I would be allowed to do if only I made a good case to the right people. So one day, I went to the access office and asked if they could help me organize a disability awareness forum for the whole school. I realized that people were not comfortable talking about disability issues. In Ghana, people with disabilities are marginalized. They are not given the opportunity to compete with abled people. So in the end, they are left at the corner to go through it all themselves. In the United States we aren't marginalized in the same way Ghanaians marginalize us, but they are afraid to ask questions about disability. They don't want to hurt your feelings by asking you questions relating to your disability. To avoid hurting your feelings, they stay away from you, which in a way is also marginalizing. I experienced this situation a lot on campus. A lot of people didn't know how to relate to me, so they chose instead to stay away from me. With that experience in my mind, I decided to use the access office to run a forum where people have the opportunity and freedom to ask any question at all about disabilities.

In a meeting with Jane Buckingham, director of disability access, I pitched the idea of having a disability forum and gave all the reasons for the forum and the various benefits it would have on those who would attend. She said, "Why not? It's a great idea, so let's do it."

In 2012, I received an invitation from the International Alliance of Women Award and in the invitation, they stated that I was a World of Difference 100 Award Winner. I was a little bit confused, "Who are these people and how do they know about me?" But when I read further into the invitation, I saw a quote from Mr. Ahedor that read, "She had been able to mobilize people with disability in the community and helped to give them a new meaning to life. Through her, a lot of people with disabilities are in school, some of them are learning a trade and others are in positions where they can raise money to look after themselves."

I know Mr. Ahedor very well. He was a tutor in Nsawam and also a person with a disability. If they could use his quote in an invitation, the award was related to some work I did while in Ghana. And indeed, the invitation went on to state that I was selected by the people of Ghana as a deserving winner because of the various projects I had done with the community of people with disabilities. Everything about the award brought great joy in my heart. The fact that I didn't know the awarding institution and the fact that I played no part in my selection meant that my work in the community hadn't been in vain. There is an eye that watches our deeds, and that eye has found me worthy to become a winner of such a prestigious award. I was overly excited.

The award ceremony was held in Washington D.C., so I had to travel there from Vermont. I remember SIT collaborated with the Ford Foundation to ensure that I traveled safely to the event. They took care of my flight arrangement and hotel reservation and even linked me with someone in Washington D.C. to help me go through the city safely and help me to travel back to Vermont. On the day of the award, when my name was mentioned, I moved to the stage with all the pride in my heart to collect my award. While on the stage, they recited all the projects I had done in my Ghanian community and I must be honest, it was on that stage that I realized that indeed, I'd come a long way in my advocacy journey. I needed that reminder to realize that yes, something had been done in the past, but a lot more needed to be done, and that award felt like the grease to my elbow—to push on and accomplish more in the future.

In June of 2013, my two-year course at SIT came to an end and the next step was graduation. I wanted my husband to be there with me to witness the day. I was so proud of what I had achieved for myself that I didn't want to go through the moment all alone. I needed him by my side, to be a witness, and to share the moment. So a few days before graduation, my husband flew from Ghana to Vermont to witness the day. The graduation wasn't the only reason I asked him to come. There was another thing.

Before completing SIT, I submitted a project to be considered for the Advancing Leaders Fellowship award at SIT. Winners of this award were given ten thousand US dollars to embark on a project of their choice in their home country. Mine was to continue my advocacy for persons with disabilities unable to access school environments in Ghana. When I submitted my project for consideration, it didn't take long before I received an email that I had been selected as a top finalist for the award. The graduation day was on the 6th of June and the Advancing Leaders Fellowship Award was on the 13th of June. I needed the moral support of my husband for both occasions.

Days before the graduation, I received an email from the director of programs. Among other things, the email stated, "You have been selected to give a commencement speech during graduation and this comes as a result of your involvement in the research that led to many retrofitting projects on campus. Are you capable of giving a speech that day?" I responded immediately, "Yes, I'm capable and I feel greatly honored to have been selected to give the commencement speech." Everything was going in my favor and I had God to thank for it all. Such recognitions make you feel seen. They make you feel like your efforts aren't in vain. It was even more special when I thought about the fact that I was a black girl in a white community who decided to push for changes.

On the graduation day, when I mounted the stage to give my speech, I said thank you to all my friends, professors, and staff. I also talked about how opened-minded and proactive the American culture was in contrast to Ghanaian culture. I complimented the school's readiness to implement changes when our research was presented to them. In terms of working around multiculturalism, equity, and inclusion, I encouraged them to continue making the changes they needed as it is a long process. Finally, I pledged on behalf of my class that we will make the necessary impacts in our communities where we find ourselves. At the end of my speech, I quoted Cesar Chavez; "Once social change begins, it cannot be reversed. You cannot uneducate the person who has learned to read. You cannot humiliate the person who feels pride. You cannot oppress the people who are not afraid anymore."

Immediately after I said the last word of the quote, the whole student congregation got up on their feet and began to clap. I smiled through it all until the sound of the clapping faded and the audience returned to their seats. I felt appreciated, and if my self-worth thermometer read 100%, after that speech, it shot up to 200%.

After graduation was the Advancing Leaders Fellowship Award. Unfortunately, there was no plane ticket for my husband since this award was not part of our initial plan. Ideally, we would go back to Ghana immediately after graduation. This is where Kim Brittainham, my former supervisor, took it upon herself to raise funding for his plane ticket. Indeed, some friends mean more than blood relations and Kim is one. She behaved just like my mother by solving all the problems I had so, I call her Mum to date. I traveled with my husband to San Francisco where the award ceremony was being held. The event was packed with people of different races and colors. I was both excited and anxious at the same time. I didn't know what was in store for me that night—whether I was going to win the award or not. Then came the time to deliver our three-minute elevator speech to a group of businessmen and corporate bodies who were present and looking for different kinds of projects to support. The idea was to win over this group of people with your elevator speech so they consider your project and invest in it. When it was my turn, I was very tense. I knew the weight of the moment and wasn't ready to let it slip. I began, "My name is Sefakor and my project is an advocacy campaign for accessible school buildings in Ghana through the media... " You could see and feel the tension all over my face and even in my voice. I had only three minutes to make a difference—to show them what my project was all about. I said, "As you see me, I'm a victim and a survivor of the lack of accessibility in school buildings. My mom used to carry me back to school every day with a container in my bag and said, 'You have to pee in this container in the classroom' because I couldn't access the toilet."

I sold them my childhood struggles and how I was ready to work hard to ensure that people with disabilities like myself wouldn't go through the challenges I went through. In the end I told them, "The impact of this project is that most people with disabilities will go to school, have employable skills, and become taxpayers to help the development of our country." The faces of the men and women present didn't give me much to be cheerful about. They had poker faces on and didn't show whether or not they fell in love with what I said.

Then came the moment of the award presentation. I was quietly seated and keenly following proceedings when my name was called as the winner of the Advancing Leaders Fellowship Award. You should have seen the cocktail of shock and happiness written all over my face. The emcee said, "Her husband traveled from Africa to support her. Let's welcome them on stage." I went up to the stage and received the award with my husband by my side. It was one of the happiest moments of our lives—a moment I would love to relive over and over again.

CHAPTER 13 QUESTIONS:

– As a transformational leader, who do you motivate your followers in the midst of all the chaos?

–What three words would you best describe leadership styles?

–You might not be a commencement speaker like me but what are the roles your friends nominated you to play?

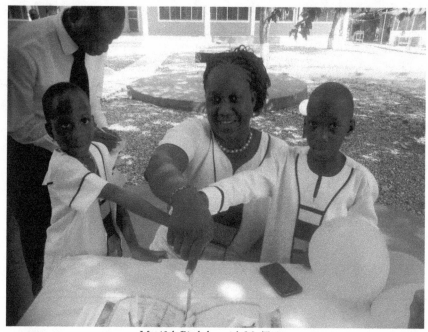

My 40th Birthday with My Twins

Put People First Campaign in Vermont

Minister for Oti Region, Hon. Joushua and
Alex during our Radio Advocacy Campaign

Minister of Education, Prof. Nana Opoku
Agyemang and Us

Int. Day for PWDs in Nsawam

Launching EEPD AFRICA

I won the National Disability Excellence Award - Ghana

AUCD International Service Award with family from Ghana to support at Washington, DC, 2018

AUCD - We All Belong Here Campaign in Washiongton DC, 2018

Mama Deb and Family

Mama Kim Rae at VCIL Office

Professor Maria Avila, Doctor Steve and Colleagues

Disability Excellence Award at the University of Vermont

ASA Presentation with my friends in academia: Prof. Geurts, Prof. Grischow and Prof. Nepveux

My USA Sch. sisters, Asma , Rebecca, and families

Ph.D Graduation with Family UVM in 2020

My son, Edonusem, and I

Chapter 14
The Devil Strikes

In July 2013, I went back to Ghana to continue working with the Ghana Education Service and also work on the project with my winnings from the Advancing Leaders Fellowship Award. I thought things would run smoothly with the project as it was structured to help people with disabilities in the country. I erroneously believed it was going to be a walk in the park and I was going to get all the necessary assistance from whoever I may need it from. The first barrier I faced was with the Registrar General's Department when I was going to register my organization.

For close to three months, I went back and forth with them and there were no clear means for me to register my organization. Sometimes I could go there and sit for the whole day and no one was ready to help or even tell me what to do to make progress. It was like walking through a maze without an escape point. I'd been in a queue for almost the whole day only to get to the desk of the department's employee and listen to them tell me, "I'm not the one to work on this. Go to the next two desks and talk to the gentleman over there." I'd walk to that gentleman's desk only to realize he wasn't at his post. In all this chaos, I saw some people walk in and skip the queue. They walked straight into an office and for the next thirty minutes, they were served. So I asked a gentleman, "What's happening here? Why do we spend forever here and don't get served but some people get here and the next minute, they are served?" He smiled and spoke in a typical local language, "This place is like that every day. If you don't know anyone inside or pay someone to push you through, only a miracle can get you through the door with your registration."

At one point, the Advancing Leaders Fellowship sent a mentor to help me get things underway and enable me to access the award funds. His name was Peter Simpson. When he came, he asked about the organization name and if I'd registered it. I told him, "I've done everything on my side to register this company but I haven't been successful with the Registrar General's Department." I showed him the organizational structure, policies, and constitution. I showed him all the paperwork concerning the organization. The only thing I didn't have was the company registration certificate from the Registrar General's Department. The following day, Peter followed me to the Registrar General's Department office. We approached one of the desks and the lady behind the desk asked courteously, "How may I help you?" I answered her, "My friend and I here want to register our organization but we seem to be having challenges we didn't anticipate from the beginning." I gave her all the documents in my possession, she looked at Peter's face, and in the next hour or so, EEPD AFRICA (Enlightening and Empowering People with Disabilities in Africa) was registered.

I asked myself, *How could something this simple take a white man before it can get done?* Peter was surprised at how fast the whole thing went. I told him, "It's because I came with a white man. My people are like that. They love taking care of strangers rather than their own. They saw your face and how white you look and decided, 'this isn't one of us, so we should serve him well.' It's like that around here."

Our first project, the Accessible School Environment Campaign, was run in Nsawam in conjunction with the Ghana National Education Campaign Coalition (GNECC). I remember Peter was still around and so involved with that project. We went around to some schools in Nsawam, assessing how accessible they were, and spoke with school authorities on the things we ought to do to make the school environment more accessible for children with disabilities. Through that campaign, EEPD AFRICA was able to grade selected school compounds, leveling the ground to aid mobility for people with disabilities. Culverts were installed and bridges were built for Adoagyiri Catholic School's students with disabilities so they could access the roads to school very easily. The advocacy part of the project took me and my team to TV and radio stations to talk and raise awareness on school accessibility issues. We were also able to meet government officials and policymakers to pitch the idea of making school accessibility important in their discussions.

In 2014, after sober reflections, something dawned on me. I looked around the space in which I'd been preaching change for the people with disabilities and asked myself, *How much has changed since I started doing this work? If today, I'm no more, what's my legacy? What would people say about me? That they saw me talking on television and heard me talking on the radio about people with disabilities? Is that all? What one big thing can I point to and say, "I did this?"* The answers to these questions didn't spark any light of joy within me. That was when I realized I needed to do more than what I was doing but then again, I sought not to be too hard on myself or see myself as a failure. I hadn't been able to make the changes I desired because people whose work it is to see to it that these changes were made did not seem eager about their responsibilities. They were the gatekeepers who will not let you in to change things and won't do anything to start the process of change either. I'd sat at too many board meetings and had had a lot of meetings with many government officials who looked like they were working for change but in the end, folded their arms and watched the status quo continue. There were instances when people in authority touted things I'd told them in private, took the praise for it, and yet did nothing thereafter. That really hurt but it didn't make me feel or think of giving up. Instead, I asked myself, *What more can I do to climb the ladder and be at the gatekeepers' level so I can force the change I want to see happen?* The answer was simple: Get more education in order to become a figure of authority in the field so I can be the one to push the agenda forward, especially when it comes to the education sector. So I decided I needed a PhD.

I remember telling my husband about it. He saw the frustration with which I spoke and said, "Take it easy on yourself. You're already doing well. If it's a PhD you want, go for it and I'll support you all the way." It feels good to know the one you call your own appreciates your work and is ready to support you. Again, when kind words like that come from your better half, it makes hard things look easier because you know, come what may, there's someone behind you who is wishing you well, praying for you, and would come to your aid if the going gets tough. The next person I needed to talk to was my mother. She had been the rock on which I stood to reach the height that I was. If there was someone whose insight was worth seeking more than anything, it was my mother.

I went to her and told her about my desire to complete a doctorate abroad. She said, "My daughter, that's a good thing. I've always known that where you are now isn't the end. There's more to do and more to accomplish. If you're ready to take the step then I support you and I can assure you of this: I don't like to travel abroad because of the cold weather but when you finally graduate with a PhD, I will put on my best Kente cloth and travel to see you graduate. It's that very day that I will look up into the sky and proclaim, 'The stone that builders refused has now become the cornerstone of the building.' I could already imagine her face covered in a light of smiles as she says that because I knew where she picked me up from when everyone said I was nothing but garbage. She was the only one who saw the light in my future when all everyone else saw was thick darkness with no light in sight. Her support that day meant a lot to me and served as the grease in my wheels and then she said again, "But this time don't travel alone. Make it a point to go with your husband and the kids. Family has a way of making heavy loads lighter when they are around you, so go with them and live together."

I started searching for the schools online. I focused on schools that had scholarship opportunities for international students. I spoke to my network of friends outside Ghana, asking them if they knew about any schools that offered scholarships for PhD programs. Many of them gave good suggestions which became my next point of search. Then I spoke to some of my former professors in Vermont, asking them about opportunities available for me to do a PhD in Vermont. I would like to believe my credentials in Vermont during my master's program helped a lot in opening doors for me. I wasn't just a woman who walked through the corridors of the school like a shadow without footprints. I was the woman who strived for excellence and advocated for changes while in Vermont. I was that woman who climbed up the stage one time to receive the International Alliance for Women Award and was selected to give a commencement speech because of my research and the positive results it brought to the school. I believed all that good work came together to make it possible for me to be considered for another schooling opportunity.

I loved Vermont so much that it felt like a home away from home. I built a lot of relationships while there and it was due to these relationships and friends who had turned family that I was eager to go to Vermont again. I wanted to meet them, shake hands with them again, and begin new relationships. When I told Rev. Nutifafa (one of our pastors from Ghana who was sent to the USA) and family about my intentions to return to Vermont, they said, "We can't wait to see you and your beautiful twins." Another friend of mine, Contompasis, said to me, "Don't worry about where you'll stay when you come around. We'll host you while you look for a permanent place." Dr. Maria Mercedez Avila said, "It would be a great thing to have you back so we can continue doing more advocacy work together."

All these assurances from friends in Vermont got my appetite whetted for the journey ahead.

Even though my letter of admission had yet to arrive, I was so sure that I was going to be given admission, that I started working to acquire a study leave without pay from the GES. Just when everything was done and I was waiting for my official admission letter with the contract from Vermont, something unexpected happened. We had gone for our Yellow Card injections, for immigration requirements at the Accra Polytechnic Hospital. From there, we went for the last review of my children at the 37 Military Hospital and that was when Dr. Odusei told me, "Due to his previous test results, your son Edonusem needs to undergo surgery in three weeks' time. This will take six or more weeks to heal and that will determine how the rest of the other surgeries will go." Saying I was devastated would be an understatement. I went through a rollercoaster of emotions, not knowing what to do or say. I asked so many questions from God; "God, why would this happen just when we are getting ready to leave this country?" No answer came, obviously. Not too long afterward, I received an email from Cynthia Gerstl-Peppin, the associate dean for academic affairs and research at UVM. The email read;

> Dear Sefakor,
>
> I hope this finds you well! As you know the admission committee was extremely impressed with your application. This is to let you know that the admissions committee voted to admit you to the PhD program in Educational Leadership and Policy Studies at UVM. Congratulations!

I spent a lot of my days waiting to receive an email from UVM congratulating me for being successful with my application. I didn't know whether or not to be happy knowing that the health situation of Edonusem would make it impossible for us to travel in the time given to us. He needed me and I had to do everything within my power to stay around him while he went through the surgery. I received Cynthia's email on the 5th of March, 2014. It took me three full days to put myself and my thoughts together to respond to the email. It was more difficult for me knowing my request for deferment could be disregarded, and thereby losing the opportunity to do my PhD with UVM, but my son's health was very critical at the moment.

When I finally gathered courage to respond to Cynthia's email I wrote...

Hi Cindy,

Thank you very much for this good news and sorry for the delay.

I am so grateful and privileged to have such a great opportunity with UVM. Thank God, I made it successfully. This message is what I have been waiting for, when I applied for this program but only God knows how I feel now. Indeed, I always pray to have the word "Congratulations" in my reply, and it came to pass. I am so grateful and so excited because this is an answered prayer. I can see, you have given me lots of time to do my PhD coursework- up to 4 years for sure and probably a 5th year. Thank you for this great offer. I will take the GTF offer.

Indeed, this is supposed to be the greatest news for me, but I have mixed feelings now. I would like to ask for a favor and some clarifications from you. Please, is there any way I can defer the course for one year, so that I start the next academic year? This request is about my five-year-old boy (one of the twins) who has been booked for three different surgeries. They were premature (7 months) when I gave birth to them, so the boy has some complications. Due to this, he is booked for the first surgery on the 23rd of April, after which the healing will determine when to do the other two. During all these surgeries, I am highly needed to be around him unlike how I left them the first time for my master's degree. I really want to plan my travel and my PhD journey after the surgery is done, when the doctors will be able to tell me the next steps on his treatment...

After sending this email, I kept my fingers crossed. Hoped. Prayed that they would see through my situation and respond positively to my deferment, and to my amazement, they granted my deferment. My son had a successful surgery and as was indicated to us earlier, it took three months for him to get well. Our lives were restored to normalcy in the months after the surgery so we started making plans to travel again in 2015. My husband had started working with his superiors to get a leave without pay so he could travel with us. I was also working with the GES to be granted a year study leave without pay, working on our visa issues, and making other travel arrangements when another trouble struck. Edonusem had to go through another round of surgery again, which according to the doctor, will take three months for him to heal completely. That meant that it wasn't possible for us to travel that year.

Cynthia sent me an email on the 11th of March, 2015 and this is what she said;

> Dear Sefakor,
>
> Thank you for your email. So glad that your son made it through the surgery well. I am writing because our challenge is that we need to make a final decision on funding for next year in the next two weeks. If you think you may not be able to start in the fall of 2015 and that perhaps waiting one more year might be best for you and your family, I can see if the graduate school will allow us to defer you for one more year. This would mean that you would start in the Fall of 2016 instead of 2015. There is no guarantee that they would let us defer for one more year but we can at least make the request if you think this might be a good idea.
>
> I hope you and your family are well!

After reading the mail, there was only one answer in my head and that was to ask for another deferment. There were no guarantees, but I wasn't scared to ask. I did once and it was granted. Twice looked far-fetched, but looking at the circumstances my family and I were in, the best solution was to ask for deferment again. So I wrote back to Cynthia and among other things, I said; "Yes, please let's try another chance to defer because we still have another surgery which will take him another six months for healing. I know this second chance will work for me and my son and God willing, we will make it next year (2016) without any hesitation." Only God knows where I got this courage of persistence from, but all I know is I pray to a living God who has a perfect plan for me.

This, too, was granted, and in 2016, all was set for us to go. Just a week before our departure, another disaster struck the family. This one came like an earth tremor that began in the silent hours of the night while the household was asleep. Everything that hung or stood in our lives came tumbling down on us. In the end, we had to get up from under the rubble, dust ourselves off, and pick up the pieces of our lives from the ground. Some broken pieces mend but you can't hide the cracks that go through them. And some pieces, no matter how hard you try, you can't put them back together. Such is my life now after that incident. I might look whole again on the outside, but on the inside, I'm just held together with a piece of tape.

My daughter Edomdedzi had returned from school on a Wednesday afternoon. Immediately after she entered the room, she came to lie on me. Something wasn't right. Her body temperature was so high I could feel it on my skin even though I was wearing clothes. I told her, "My daughter, you're very warm. This is not normal. Take off your uniform, go into the bathroom, and take a shower. That should lower your body temperature." She said, "Mom, I'm not sick. I'm very fine." I insisted until she went to the bathroom and took the shower. Moments after she returned from the shower, her temperature got worse. I bundled her up, put her in the car, and drove her to the hospital. They checked her and did some tests which came back negative but her temperature was still super high. The doctor gave us some drugs and said, "Take her home and give her the drugs. The temperature should come down by tomorrow morning."

When we came home that night, we couldn't sleep. I spent the whole night squeezing water out of towels and placing it on her. And no matter how wet the towel was, it dried mere minutes after I placed it on her. She wasn't eating nor drinking anything and that got me very worried. Immediately after the morning light came, I brought her back to the hospital. They checked her up again and detected nothing. She was put on a drip and all day nothing was changing for the better. Her temperature kept going up. At some point during the day, I called my husband and told him what was happening. He came to the hospital too and saw things for himself. I remember that when the night came, the situation hadn't changed. I couldn't sleep at the hospital because of how inaccessible the place was, so my husband stayed behind at the hospital to help our daughter through the night.

The next morning, when I came back to the hospital, I realized my daughter was turning blue. Her skin color had dulled and was changing from fair to blue. My husband said her line for fluid and injections got disconnected from the hand the whole night and they could not reset it. According to them, they have an expert who sets the lines, and he will come in the morning at 9am. That means, the whole night no fluid entered her body. You could see the color of her veins through her skin and she had become weaker than she was when I'd left her the night before. I told my husband and the nurses around, "My daughter is turning blue." They all looked at her and didn't see what I was talking about. Maybe it was because they had spent all night with her and seen her throughout the night so they couldn't easily spot the changes in her. I did and it got me worried, so I told the nurses on duty, "I want her to be referred to 37 Military Teaching Hospital. That's where her brother goes to see a doctor whenever there is a problem. I think the doctor there will know what the issue is." They didn't think my daughter's issue was so dire that she had to be referred. They told me they couldn't. One said, "This is not a case to be referred to the 37 Military Hospital. It's something we can handle. Just be patient." I wasn't ready to listen to them. I insisted. At this point, my husband had a call from their immigration office demanding that he report to work so he left the hospital. I was a lone wolf insisting that the right thing be done. Later, my husband's cousin, Aunty Dzifa, joined me to run errands until the end of the day.

It took them three hours to prepare a referral note for my daughter to be transferred. When we were all set to move, there was no ambulance to carry my daughter. I told them, "You don't worry, we will drive her there ourselves." They said, "It's a referral case so you can't drive the patient personally to the referral hospital. An ambulance has to do it." They started making calls to other hospitals, enquiring if there were any ambulances available. Later, they said they had one that was coming from Haatso. It took the ambulance more than two hours to reach the Nsawam Hospital. They hurriedly placed my daughter in the ambulance. I also got in and it moved. Aunty Dzifa and our prophetess, Abigail, took a car and followed us. Immediately after we started the journey, I started calling all the doctors I knew in the pediatric section at 37 about our journey to them. We met very heavy traffic on the road from Nsawam to Accra, so it took us over two hours to get to the hospital. When we arrived, a team of pediatricians rushed to the ambulance, opened the door, quickly removed my daughter, placed her on a stretcher, and rushed her into the ward. Before I got down from the ambulance, they were already inside the ward attending to her. Dzifa and Abigail stayed outside praying as I was the only one allowed to stay inside. For more than three hours these doctors stood by my daughter doing everything possible to bring her to health, but their efforts couldn't save the life of my daughter. All of the sudden, I saw the team around her lower their heads in unison. I asked, "What's wrong? What happened?" The lead doctor said calmly, "We lost her. She died."

I can't stop crying even as I write this. My mouth was wide open, but I couldn't utter a word. My heart kept beating loudly as if being pushed out of my chest. I looked through the spaces between the team and found her lying lifeless with her eyes opened. I screamed out loud, "Is that how we die?" One of the doctors ran her palm over my daughter's face and shut her eyes. Everything played out like a movie right before my eyes. How could my daughter die just like that? A few days ago, she stood in the church and sang her heart out as she did on every Sunday. After her song ministration she announced to the church, "This is my last Sunday worship with you. I'm traveling to America!" The whole church laughed and clapped. At seven years, she could raise her voice in worship to the Lord and the whole church would come to a standstill. How could she die like that? This is a girl who hadn't been sick since the day she was born. Always strong and bubbly. But one day she ran a temperature and she was gone like powder in the wind.

I looked at the doctor's face and then back at the body of my daughter and said, "No, she's not dead. My daughter can't die. Something is wrong somewhere." All those present couldn't believe that I could say my daughter wasn't dead. They looked at me with disbelief in their eyes, but I was so convinced in my spirit that my daughter wasn't dead. Dead bodies go cold but my daughter's body was still very warm and that increased my assurance that she wasn't dead. Days after their birth I had been declared dead and was prepared for the mortuary. The dawn before I was going to the mortuary, I coughed and came back to life. If it happened to me, it could happen to my daughter too. If they made a mistake with me, they could make a mistake with my daughter, too. So, I repeated, "No, my daughter isn't dead. I'm very sure of that. Give us some time. Don't send her to the mortuary now. Give us at least three days and God will do His miracle." The doctor was very kind to me. He said, "It's against the policy of the profession to keep the dead among the living, but if you insist, we'll keep her in a separate room for the next three days. You have to come around every day to keep an eye on her."

I called my husband, told him what had happened, and he said, "I know Edomdedzi isn't dead. She'll come back to life." I called my pastor, Rev. Gbortsyo, who has prayed with us from day one, and told him about the current confirmation from the doctors. I requested that we, as a church, fast for three days and pray for my daughter. I said the same to my family, too; for the next three days, it was going to be about fasting and prayers. I remember some family and friends thought I was going crazy. They told my husband and my mom to have me checked; maybe I was going through some psychological imbalance. That didn't stop me from believing in the healing and restoration powers of the Almighty God. We kept praying and fasting each day and each morning, my husband and some family members would go to the hospital, sit next to her body, and pray. On the second day of fasting and prayers a pastor from my sister's church called my sister and told her about a revelation he had received about my daughter. He said, "Your daughter spoke to me in a revelation. She requested that her father and some family members go to her body and pray for her, and when they get to her body, they should turn her counterclockwise until her head is positioned where her legs are resting currently."

My sister Selorm was shocked to hear that. The pastor continued, "When they enter the room where she lays, they'll see a sign. Her body won't be warm again but she will be sweating. That indicates that she's indeed coming back to life." When my sister told us about this revelation, the whole family was instantly thrown into an ecstatic mood. My husband, my brother Seyram, and our prayer leader Anthony dressed up immediately and drove towards the hospital. I wasn't able to go with them so I stayed behind with a heart full of prayers, hope for a miracle, and a desire to see my daughter back to life so I could hug her again. According to my husband, when they arrived she was indeed sweating so they all joined hands and prayed for her and then later turned her head as instructed to where her feet were resting. They prayed again and again, for several hours, but nothing happened. They came home. The next day was the third day. We prayed and prayed and prayed, again no change. The three days I requested were exhausted and nothing came out of it. There, I remembered 1 John 5:14:15 which reminded me, that if what we ask is according to His will, He hears us. Edomdedzi continued lying lifeless on the bed. She was prepared and sent to the mortuary.

The next day, May 4th of 2016, I sent an email to UVM copying all other people who were expecting my arrival in the US. I wrote;

Dear All,

I am with a heavy heart to announce to you that I just lost my only daughter Edomdedzi H.Y. Pomeyie. She was running temperature for less than a week (three days) and she was admitted to the hospital. She came back from school on Wednesday 27th, and was super hot. After she took some cold water, she became extremely hot, so I sent her to the hospital. They tested her and said she had no problem despite the high temperature, so we came home. I couldn't sleep the whole night so we went back on Thursday. Things became so serious and we requested for a transfer from Nsawam hospital on Friday morning to 37 Military Hospital in Accra, the capital. Three hours after arriving there, she was confirmed dead in front of me. I didn't believe it, so I asked for some three days prayers for her to wake her up which we did in our church. But she couldn't wake up until today. SHE DIED ON LAST FRIDAY 29TH April, 2016 AND WILL BE BURIED ON FRIDAY 13TH MAY. Attached is her picture. This is the worst thing I could ever think of happening because this is her first time falling sick and going to the hospital. She used to lead the twin brother to the hospital but has never fallen sick for the past seven years now. Nobody knows what killed her because all the tests couldn't confirm any specific sickness. I am still not ACCEPTING THIS, but it did happen to me. O God, I lost my daughter just like that??? Hmmm, please keep me in your prayers because this is too much for me. I am so devastated and hopeless because she is my everything especially during the times of hardship, she would sing to calm us down in the family. As young as she was, she was singing at our church and leading the Sunday school children in signing.

After my daughter was buried, I asked myself, "What's the worst that could happen to me again? What pain haven't I gone through already? Will I allow this to stop me from pursuing my goals in life?" The answer was simply this: NO! I started setting up my sail against the wind so I could begin from where I left off. We were waiting to hear from my husband's work and whether or not his leave without pay application would be granted. Unfortunately, they responded in the negative. That meant he couldn't leave with us to the US. He said to me, "It's alright. You two should go now. I'll make arrangements to visit you from time to time."

In July of 2016, Edonusem and I packed our things, said goodbye to family and friends, and set off to the United States of America. Did that help me forget about the loss of my daughter? Did that make the pain less heavy than it used to be? No, it didn't. Every now and then I remembered her and how we used to be. Her smiles never faded from my memories and her voice when she sang was deeply etched on the walls of my memories. I thought of her sometimes and I developed goosebumps on my skin. I talked about her and I would cry with how deeply I missed her. I still believe she is resting and I will definitely meet her again as the word of God says in 1 Thessalonians 4:13-18: "But we do not want you to be uninformed, brethren, about those who are asleep, so that you will not grieve as do the rest who have no hope. For if we believe that Jesus died and rose again, even so God will bring with Him those who have fallen asleep in Jesus."

CHAPTER 14 QUESTIONS:

–Death is inevitable and as you can see, a part of me is buried but I am still alive. I know the doctors tried their best, but nobody controls death. How do you perceive death and what can you do to keep going if death strikes your house?

–Do you think that some death could be prevented if we had the best machines to diagnose, medications, and experts in the medical field on the ground?

–How do you manage grief and what is your source of grief management?

Chapter 15
A New Life

We got to the USA knowing very well where we were going to live temporarily. Even though the Contompasis are ready for us, I was looking for a place that was closer to campus and accessible but since I couldn't find such a place before coming, I arranged to spend some time with Rev. Nutifafa, a family pastor who lived in New York. When we got to the airport, it was Rev. Nutifafa who came to meet us and brought us to his house in New York. We stayed with him and his family for two to three weeks while looking for accessible housing in Vermont. After those three weeks, we still couldn't find any accessible housing close to campus. School was about to start so I couldn't continue living in New York. We needed to travel to Vermont.

After so many days, we still couldn't find any housing that was accessible enough for me. It was during that time that I spoke to Doctor Stephen Contompasis, (whom we now call Uncle Steve for short) a medical doctor who lived in Vermont and with whom I'd struck up an acquaintance with while I was doing my master's at SIT. I knew him through Prof. Mercedes Maria Avila when she brought me to train the medical department in UVM on cultural competency. He had been behind the scenes in all our journeys since I made up my mind to come back to do my PhD. In fact, he was very instrumental in all our plans for the second coming to the USA. He knew I was struggling to find accessible housing around campus, so he decided to host us. So, one day, Uncle Steve came to New York to visit us and to see where we lived in New York. When he confirmed that his wife and children were ready to welcome us, we were so excited. He was very clear in his words that, "You can come along and see where we live and then decide if it would be conducive for you to live with us. If it is, you can stay with us for some time while you continue searching for accessible housing."

We packed bag and baggage and the following day, we joined Uncle Steve in his car for the six-to-seven-hour journey to Burlington, Vermont. I just want to let you know that he is a pure white man so not all the whites see blacks differently. He and his family has been so kind to us till today.

We came with him that day to his house. He lived in a very big house in a white community just fifteen minutes away from UVM. He was living with his wife and his daughter—the youngest of his five children. When we got to his house, he showed me the staircase leading to the rooms and asked if it would be easy for me to climb to the rooms upstairs. I got out of my wheelchair, put my two hands on the floor, and started crawling up the stairs. Uncle Steve was traumatized to see me climb the stairs the way I was doing. He covered his eyes with his two palms and all the while screaming, "Oh nooo, that can't happen. That's too much for you. I can't watch you go through this every day while you live around here. His wife was equally thrown into shock and emotional pain immediately. I put my two palms on the floor and started making my way up the stairs. She turned away. She couldn't look at me. They thought going up that way demeaned me and wasn't a good sight to behold. I told them, "This is very normal for me. I've gone through that almost all my life. Anytime I get to a place where my crutches can't go or my scooter can't access, I put gloves on my hands and crawl until I get to the top." Uncle Steve shook his head in disbelief and his wife couldn't shake the sight off her eyes so she continued wearing that face of disbelief when she saw me crawl.

When we finally got to the sitting room, Mrs. Contompasis (Aunty Mary for short) sat next to me and started a conversation. She asked about life and the journey back to Vermont. She asked about the challenges I'd faced since I came and how I was dealing with those challenges. Before I could open my mouth and answer her questions, I saw Uncle Steve and some friends from the neighborhood carrying wood, carpentry tools, and other stuff into the house. All I heard in the next moments were the sounds of a striking hammer and people discussing where to put what and how to fix what. In just under an hour, Uncle Steve and his friends had built a ramp in the house for me. He came up and said to me, "We've fixed a ramp. Would you like to come and try it?" I used my wheelchair on it and it was okay. He asked again, "You think it's okay?" I responded, "Yeah, it's okay. Not too steep and that means I can wheel myself up and down without anybody's help."

He showed us our room. He said, "This used to be our eldest daughter's room. She's married and now lives in Italy. You can live here until you're able to sort out your housing issues." I thanked him and told him how grateful we were for such kindness from him and his wife. Somedays I stood outside watching the vicinity and how plush it looked.

Two other friends, Deborah-Lisi Baker and Kim Brittainham, who I call my American mothers and who have been so instrumental in my journey, had not stopped searching for accessible housing. Who thinks about this situation in America? That I will be searching for accessible housing in America which is the home of the brave and land of the free? They did all that they could but to no avail. I could remember while I was in Ghana, Mama Deb even sent me some application forms so I'd know how the processes would be. They had both worked with the Vermont Center for Independent Living before, and that was why they knew all about the housing processes, but still I could not get accessible housing. There were obstacles here and there, which were very interesting to discover, due to my status as a black woman with a physical disability and a family. My application was never accepted in some of the housing companies because of the systemic policy structures. They thought they could help me just as they did to other Americans with disabilities but that was not the case, therefore, they were so frustrated. To some housing agents, I am not a citizen, hence I cannot get housing from them. To other housing companies, I have a family, but they were looking for tenants who are single. Mama Deb and her husband David were even ready to pay for my first three months' rent but there was no available accessible housing for me and my son. She ended up buying a scooter for me to use to get to campus while living with the Contompasis family. That was how far they went to help me. Mama Deb and Mama Kim have been super helpful to us to this day. I call them my destiny changers because they will go any extra mile to make things work for us. Indeed, I can never thank these two women enough because they are in indeed true mothers with pure hearts.

Everyone I saw around was white, and judging by their appearances and their way of life, they were people who were well-to-do. I was on my way to school once when a woman stopped me with a conversation; "Excuse me, do you live around here?" I responded, "Yeah, I live around here." She queried further, "Where?

Which house do you live in?" I responded, "I live with the Contompasis family." She said, "Aww really? You live with the Contompasis family?" The look on her face when she said that was one of disbelief mixed with discomfort. Her demeanor sought to say, "Who the hell are you to live among us?" Clearly, she wasn't pleased to see me around their neighborhood, and she made it clear with the way she acted when I told her where I lived.

I had come a long way and had met too many hardships to allow that stranger's behavior to worry me. The most important thing was how well we were treated and taken care of by the Contompasis. When my son needed a school, the choice was between public school and private school. I thought of sending him to a public school because it was fee-free, but Uncle Steve said no. One day, he went out with my son and when they came back, my son had already been admitted to a private school close by. He is a staunch catholic, and according to him, all their donations went into that school, so it was easier to get admission there for him. In the mornings, I prepared my son's meal for school and Uncle Steve would drive him to school before going to work. In the afternoon, when school closed around 2:30pm, he would go and pick him up from the school and bring him back home while I was in school studying. Sometimes I would get home late in the evening but by the time I got home, Uncle Steve and his wife, Aunty Mary had already tucked him in and he was sleeping. Wherever Uncle Steve went, he went with my son Edonusem, so he became very well known in the community. That was when a neighbor became friends with my son. He was an old man in his late sixties.

He came around the house often to play with my son in the backyard. Sometimes he came with new toys for him and both of them would play football, frisbee, and sometimes hockey. According to this neighbor, he liked Edonusem so much because he helped him stay active all the time. Their friendship was something I admired. It was like the old blending with the new. Maybe the man looked at Edonusem and saw the beginning of his life flashing before his eyes. In my mind, my son reminded him of when he was young, and so he decided to come around to play with him so he could catch up with his young life. They would play and shout out of excitement and it was exciting to know he had a friend in a community other people thought we were not worthy to belong in.

One day, Uncle Steve and his wife had to travel to Italy for one week. Their daughter had given birth and they wanted to go and spend some time with her and the family. We had to make plans on who would take Edonusem to school while they were away. To me, it was very simple. I told Uncle Steve, "Edonusem's friend lives just across the street. We can have a word with him so he'll take him to school and bring him back when school closes." Uncle Steve asked, "You mean that man who comes here to play with the boy?" I responded, "Yeah." Uncle Steve burst into laughter. He said, "You expect so much from that man. You think he'll do that? Not in a million years would he consider taking this boy to school." I protested, "Uncle Steve, they are friends—very good friends. He comes here to play with him and he's always excited when he's around Edonusem. He'll gladly agree to do that since it gives him more opportunities to be with the boy." Uncle Steve asked, "You want to try? Go to him and ask him. I'll be here waiting for you."

I set off to the man's house, with all the hope in my heart that he was going to say yes to my request. When I got to his house, he was there with his wife. They welcomed me and asked what brought me to their house. I said, "Your friend needs help and I'm hoping you could help." He answered, "Sure. What kind of help?" I told him, "Uncle Steve is traveling for a week, and I'll need you to pick Edonusem from school at 2:45pm and ensure that he eats his food because he doesn't like eating. I'll return from school by 8:30pm and pick him up from here." The man looked at my face sternly and said, "I don't think I can bargain for this." I was shocked. I told him, "It's your friend we are talking about here. Edonusem. The boy you come to play with every now and then." He repeated his answer, "Yes, I know, but I don't think I can bargain for that." His wife chipped in, "I want to understand. You mean we have to pick him up from school and ensure that he eats his food. Are you going to prepare his food?" I responded, "Yeah, I will do everything. I will take him to school in the morning and you'll pick him up in the afternoon and ensure he eats his food and stay here with him until I come back for him in the evening."

The wife nodded her head for a while and said, "I think we can try?" The man got furious about his wife suggesting that they should give it a try. He retorted, "I would never dare cross that road with that boy!" I was stunned. I didn't even know what else to say or do. All of the sudden, his expression changed from receptive to angry. I said apologetically, "I'm sorry. I didn't know my request would upset you in this way. It will never happen again. Forgive me." They were both seated quietly and were looking at me. I turned my scooter around and drove away. That day I understood racism in a different light, but most importantly, it made me understand the kind of heart the Contompasis family had to be able to accommodate us for a whole year. Someone wouldn't hold the hand of my son and cross the road with him, but Uncle Steve and his family took us in and gave us a perfect environment to thrive.

After struggling for a whole year without finding accessible housing, I finally got in touch with Goma Mabika, a Congolese national who was also an international student. I got to know Goma through Dr. Mercedez Avila. Before coming to UVM, Avila told me, "There's a Congolese international here called Goma. He is already in the PhD program and also an African. So just in case you need an African perspective about the program, you can talk to Goma and he'll always be ready to help." Now, during my fruitless search for disability friendly accommodation, I got to know from Asma, my friend and classmate, that there was an empty space in the building where Goma lived. The only problem was that the empty room was on the third floor of the building and there was no lift facility in the building. I made enquiries about the availability of the space and how much ought to be paid. I was assured it was available and would be offered to me if I was ready. I knew I couldn't use it but because of how desperate my situation was, I had to negotiate with Goma for him to move to the top of the building so I could take up his space at the ground floor. It wasn't easy for me to discuss these issues with him, knowing very well that he also lived with his wife and his two children and such a move could cause inconvenience for them in so many ways. I was desperate. The Contompasis were thinking of selling their house. Their kids had grown and left the house, leaving only the two of them. They no longer had any use for that big house. They were selling it so that they could move into a smaller place. I didn't want to be the reason they keep living in that house and incurring losses.

I went to see Goma one day with Uncle Steve and discussed the issue with him. I told him, "You already know my story and how for the whole one year I've been moving up and down looking for a place. It hasn't been easy and I keep running out of luck. I need you to help me this time." I told him about the space upstairs and my plan to get him to move up so I could occupy the ground floor. Uncle Steve also chipped in, pleading with Goma to do it on humanitarian grounds. Goma said, "No problem at all. I can take it. All I need is some time to get ready; get my things together and move." His acceptance actually didn't surprise me at all. I knew his heart and I knew he would do it for me. I was only concerned about the inconvenience I was putting him and his family through. We gave ourselves three months to sort things out and finally moved. When the three months was up, rent for the top rooms had been increased, but Goma didn't complain. He paid the difference so he and his family could move there. This is how deeply the

American system fails those of us with systemic barriers. Can you imagine this type of swapping happening in America? Nobody will believe this struggle if I tell my people in Ghana, or Africa in general, that we are still struggling for our rights to have equal and equitable access to basic needs in America. You can easily know that some policies are not connected to practical life on the ground. You can also notice the communal life of Africans exhibited by Goma. This tells you the individualistic ideology or individual comfort is not entertained in African culture. I am not sure if any American would go that extra-mile to pay more rent even if they were also a student like me.

It's not easy to find people who are ready to make sacrifices for you, especially when those people are not your family, not people you call friends, or not people who knew you from your beginning. So when you finally find them and they agree to put their comfort on the side just so you can be comfortable, you appreciate them with all your heart and the memories of their deeds go with you until the end. Today, I still live in the space Goma left for me because there's nowhere else to move to. All the housing around this area is either not wheelchair accessible or the ones that are accessible are only open to U.S. citizens in terms of finance, SSI, or insurance status. People like me, who are foreigners, can't gain access to the systems that manage these facilities.

Indeed, I have some professors who have visible and invisible disabilities who fought with me, and I took courses like Culture of Disability, Collaborative Consultation, Policy and Practices, Educational Leadership, Survey, Qualitative Research, etc. but I still need the hand of an African to put all these into reality for me. The spirit of family and community building is inherent in most Africans, and no one can take that from them.

How Mom Finally Took Her Bow

Mom started complaining of minor sickness when she went home for retirement. I would call her one day and she would say, "Sefakor, I've not been feeling well lately at all. As I'm talking to you right now, my feet are sticky. When I put my foot down and begin to walk, it becomes uneasy for me to lift one foot after another. It touches the ground and it's stuck, like I'd stepped on chewing gum." I called my siblings to discuss it with them and in no time, they took her to the hospital. We moved her from one hospital to another but nothing changed. If anything, she kept complaining of new sicknesses. I remember one day after talking to her, she said, "My feet. They feel like they've been placed in a burning flame. They keep burning me and I can't do anything to stop it." Again, I called my siblings and told them about it. Hospital after hospital, nothing changed.

The most surprising thing about her situation was that, after complaining about her feet burning and getting sticky, the next time you talk to her, you'll hear her say something like, "I attended the wedding ceremony of this family member or that family friend." We got confused. Her legs were burning and sticky yet she was able to attend weddings and travel with pastors to administer communions to the sick and pray for them. What really was the issue? We all concluded that her suffering was a result of menopause. When she complained, we told her, "Mom, don't worry. These are all symptoms of menopause. You'll be fine."

One evening, after complaining about these same issues to me, I called my sister and told her to bring our mother to live with her so she could rest and visit the hospital for consistent check-ups in Accra. At first, she didn't want to travel to Accra. My mom was like that. She always had a reason not to travel and leave her home behind, no matter how flimsy that excuse sounded. But we were determined to bring her to Accra and put her on soft house arrest so she could rest and get medical help. Finally, she agreed to travel, and when she got to Accra, she was sent to Ridge hospital. The doctors ran a lot of tests on her which all came back negative. She was sent back home to continue her medication. A few weeks later, she started complaining of constipation. There was no purgative she didn't take and there was no medical care she wasn't given, and the constipation persisted. One day when she was taken to the hospital, I called the doctor and begged him to admit my mother and run a comprehensive check on her to see what was wrong. I was getting worried and I was determined to put an end to her incessant complaints of illness. The doctor didn't believe he ought to admit her because of constipation. But he finally did when my mother's blood pressure shot up abnormally. She was stable after some time and in the morning, when I was preparing to write my comprehensive exams, a call came in from my youngest sister Selorm. She said, "Sefakor, Mom has died."

I was so shocked I didn't know what to say. "Mom died? From what? What killed her? She only had constipation. How could constipation kill Mom?" She said, "Yeah, I guess it's her time." I was shattered and for many minutes I thought the whole thing was just a dream. I kept looking around, looking for a sign to tell me it was a dream. I was waiting for someone or something to wake me up from the nightmare I was having. Tick-tock, tick-tock, the time moved. Nothing changed. I touched my cheeks and said, "Wow, it's all real. So, my mom, too, is gone?" To date, I haven't been able to come to terms with the death of my mother, especially when I think of what killed her. But surprisingly, Mom knew her time was due. She saw the dying days of her time and made arrangements before the final bell tolled. A few minutes after Selorm announced her death to me, she sent me a photo of a list of names and said, "Sefakor, please hold on to this for me before I get disorganized." I asked what that was and she said, "Mom gave me this list and instructions on what to do when she dies."

The list contained the names of people she had worked with during her lifetime. Most of them were pastors. All of the names on the list had been assigned roles. For instance, she wrote, "Call this pastor, Rev. Opare when I die. I've already arranged with him to preach during my funeral." On another name she wrote, "No matter where I die, call this pastor, Rev. Adeve, and tell him I'm dead. He'll arrange for my body to be sent back to Sogakope." And for my part she said, "... And don't bury me until Sefakor is here. She should be at my funeral at any cost."

Immediately after she was sent to the mortuary, we started calling all the people on the list. All of them confirmed the arrangements my mother made with them and started doing the things they promised her they would when she died. We called Rev. Adeve, the pastor who was supposed to transfer my mother's body back to Sogakope. Immediately after we told him about the death of my mother, he said, "Oh, she's gone?" He was shocked and sad at the same time. He said, "I owe her a duty and I would do just as I promised her." He arranged for the body to be carried back to Sogakope morgue. All other arrangements were put in place for the burial of my mother. On my part, I couldn't come to Ghana immediately. I had exams to write so I told the family to give me some time to finish writing the exams and get ready to return to Ghana.

My mom died on the 26th of May, 2018, but they had to wait until July for me to return for her burial. In her tribute, we wrote, "Indeed, nobody can replace you and this is the significance of a mother's death. We have now come to that understanding that you're irreplaceable in our lives. You said it but we took it for granted." It's said that we only have to lose what we have before we get to know how valuable that thing was. In our eyes, our mother was valuable and played a part nobody could play in our lives. We appreciated her for that. The only sad thing was that we didn't know she was going to leave us so soon. At sixty-eight, we thought we would see more days with her so we could continue pouring adoration on her for the things she did in our lives, but death had a plan and that plan ensured we lost her when we didn't expect to. Indeed, we miss the prayers of our mother to date.

I still remember the lessons, especially the one where I had to look through the mirror to see who I really was. It was that lesson that opened my eyes to who I could become if only I took my education seriously, and with the help of God, I am here today, striving to become a doctor in academia all because one morning Mom held a mirror to me and asked me to look through and see who I was. Knowing who I was helped me to bring out who I could be. When she quoted Isaiah 43:2 and said, "When you pass through the waters, God will be with you," I knew I had a protector who would be with me through thick and thin. All I had to do was to commit my ways to him. I did and see where God has brought me. He hasn't finished with me yet, but for how far He has brought me I'm grateful, and it was all due to a mother who saw a future nobody could dream about and ensured I got there no matter what.

CHAPTER 15 QUESTIONS:

−What does a mother mean to you?

−What role does she play in your life?

−What keeps your umbilical cord alive even if you are disconnected from your mother?

−Do you believe life is generally spiritual and everyone is a spiritual being?

Chapter 16
The Way Forward

On March 11th, 2020, I presented my dissertation at a time when COVID-19 was threatening to bring everything to a standstill. Some call it luck, but I call it the hand of God at play. In the moment I had to do my presentation, we looked around for my supervising professor, but she was nowhere to be found. The process of dissertation presentation is such that your professor has to introduce you to the gathering before you can start the presentation. What it means is that one cannot present until their supervising professor has finished introducing them. Fifteen minutes had passed and still my supervisor was nowhere to be found. People started placing calls to her phone and leaving voice messages asking about her whereabouts. Soon, someone got her on the phone, and she said, "I'm late because I had to fight to ensure that Sefakor is able to do her presentation today."

We didn't understand her statement until she told us what was really happening. As we were all seated waiting to start the presentation, there were meetings going on, and their agenda was to shut down the school at exactly 2 o'clock that day. What it meant was that all activities, including my presentation, had to stop. It took the intervention of my supervising professor, Katie Shepherd, to ensure that my presentation goes on before the shutdown notice was sent. She was able to negotiate for some time for me but we had to do everything in a rush to avoid being cut off mid-presentation.

I had forty-five minutes to finish the presentation so others would have ten or fifteen minutes to ask questions. After everything, I had to send my forms to various departments for them to sign, indicating that I'd finished my dissertation. It was a huge race against time, but I had to do it. I drove my scooter, moving from office to office, hurriedly asking the authorities to append their signatures on my forms per the normal process. Luckily, they all did. A few moments after I submitted the form and it was filed as complete, an email dropped from the school administration ordering the school to shut down due to the COVID-19 pandemic!

I gave a huge sigh of relief and said to God, "You always come through for me. Indeed, you make all things beautiful in your own time, Ecclesiastes 3:11. Thank you so much, Lord." If that moment passed me by, if I wasn't able to present my dissertation at the said date, a lot of things would have gone against me. It would have affected my scholarship and the thoughts of it all would have put me in a very dicey situation. I would have missed the presence of all the good friends and family members who were present. We didn't know when the school was going to be reopened and that meant I wouldn't have known the exact time I would have the opportunity again to present my dissertation. My dissertation won the best dissertation award. Indeed, nothing good comes easy. In the end, the juice was indeed worth the squeeze.

One night when I was alone and reflecting on how far life had brought me, I thought of Mom and her promise to be here with me on my graduation day. I remembered how she said it; "I don't like to travel abroad because of the cold weather but when you finally graduate with PhD, I will put on my best white Kente cloth and travel to see you graduate." I said in my head, "See how things turned out? I'm here, but Mom is not here. Even if she was alive, her wish of traveling to see me graduate wouldn't have come through because of this pandemic." That night I asked myself the question my mom would have loved to ask if she was alive; "So Sefakor, what next?" She always wanted to know the next step and the next height I was ready to conquer.

I didn't want that question to go unanswered. Though Mom wasn't there to ask the question, I thought I needed the answer for myself. That's how growth happens. You assess your yesterday, aware of your today, so you can determine where your next step will take you. "What's next?" is an easy question for me to answer because even before the PhD journey started I had a clear plan of what to do next and what not to do. What to do next is always going to be the continuation of my advocacy project but with a different touch.

Some years ago, a community cheaply sold to me a huge tract of land as their contribution to a dream I harnessed long ago. The dream is to build an inclusive education complex for all people with disabilities. In my experience with the Ghana education system, one of the greatest obstacles that impede people with disability to pursue education at any level is accessibility. I've been there before, suffered the consequences, and I'm here today as a witness to the difficulties and pains one has to go through to access education as a person with a disabilities. I don't wish that to continue forever. We've talked about it, demonstrated against it, and sat on hundreds of board meetings trying to make a change, but in the end, nothing happens.

This is the time for someone to take the issue up and cause a change to happen, because all persons, no matter their situation in life, deserve education in an environment where their safety and peace of mind is assured. So my dream is all about building a one stop facility for the education of all people with disabilities not only in Ghana, but for people from neighboring countries, too.

I'd had the dream since childhood to leave a legacy for posterity. I can remember how some of my course-mates—Rebecca, Asma, Faith, Mika, and some other professors—were pulled to my vision. Rebecca and Faith took it upon themselves to work with me day and night to make a video for my fundraising. Little did I know I am not allowed to raise funds as an international student. That was another big blow for my dream even though they were ready to support and share my fundraising link. This was another eye opener for them as Americans because they did not know what we go through as international students. All the same, I still believe this dream will be achieved through other means because I will work toward it.

It's hard looking at the resources involved to be able to achieve such a dream but I'm not ready to use that as an excuse to give up. My life was hard. Starting as a girl carried on my mother's back to school, given a can to urinate in class due to the inaccessible nature of our washrooms to falling down stairs of different heights and now to where I am today. It hasn't been easy, but giving up wasn't in my psyche so I soldiered on until I reached where I am today. Nothing has been easy for me. That's why the almost impossible nature of my dreams does not scare me. I'm ready. I will ask. I will beg. I'll pray. I'll succeed so the child with disabilities whose horizon is to end up in the street as a beggar can have an education and dreams that transcend the streets. But I have a message for parents who have kids with different forms of disabilities.

Message to Parents with Children with Disabilities

You take on a great commitment the day you have a child with a disability. The dream to build an inclusive education school for all kids with disabilities is yet to materialize, but we can't wait until it's ready, so we go and dump our kids there as a way of escaping the responsibilities of taking care of them. There's no escape in raising a child with a disability. If a parent won't run from raising an abled child, then why run from raising a child with disabilities? So, the whole thing starts from a shift in perspective. Society, especially the African society, places little value on the child with a disability. Some even see it as a form of a curse as a result of our bad deeds. But that perception has to change. We need to embrace our kids with disabilities with the same open arms we use to embrace the other ones. When we embrace them for who they are and accept their limitations while opening their eyes to their abilities, they'll thrive just like their counterparts.

Children feed on the energy of their parents. When you're excited about them and accept them for who they are, they automatically accept themselves and begin to shine inward until their lights begin to spread. When my dad left us, a light in me went off. I felt dejected. I felt unworthy of love and I felt this guilt even as a child. It took the hands of my mother to mold a different spirit in me. She showed me off. She gave me work to do. She took me to places and told me I was worthy. She said I could do it and indeed pushed me to do it. When I was successful at doing something, no matter how small, she celebrated in a way that made me feel like I belonged. When I failed at something, she never associated it with my disability. She only corrected me and said, "Next time, you'll do it right; don't worry."

So when I went to school and everyone else taunted me and teased me about my situation, I had the strength to face them, and even the days that I had no strength left, I knew I had love somewhere from someone waiting to embrace me and say, "Sefakor, you're worthy. That's why you're in the same school as them." It's these acts of kindness and love from my mom that fueled my light so I could stay shining when everyone else's light was dimming on me.

I'm a Christian, so when it comes to something to believe in, I always choose God. But I'm not oblivious to the fact that other people have other things they believe in. So I say to parents who have kids with disabilities to hold fast to whatever they believe in. When the going gets tough and rough, it's our faith in the supernatural that keeps us going. I got to know from my childhood that I am a child of God but not a mistake. My Mum used the Bible verse "Before I formed thee in the belly, I knew thee; and before thou camest forth out of the womb I sanctified thee, and I ordained thee a prophet unto the nations." Jeremiah 1:5. My mom never stopped reminding me of God and how he'd become our strength. So when others rejected us and mocked us for being cursed, we held the belief that there is a hand big enough to embrace us and cover us from the shame of the world. And it was those hands that guided us every step of the way. I've never shied away from mentioning God and dedicating my success to him because I see him in every step I take. In fact, at times I have to remind myself with some of the Bible verses when the going gets tough. A typical day I can remember was when I had to give God a seat in my prayer closet to ask Him questions about Jeremiah 29:11. After praying with this verse, I was satisfied, and my spirit was at peace. As a parent, you need special strength and grace to accept and push your child with a disability to a higher height, and that strength and grace can only come from the supernatural, so you can't ignore it. Don't forget: life is spiritual!

To the Person with any Form of a Disability

I have a message for you to deliver to the world. Tell everyone you meet that, I say, DISABILITY IS PART OF HUMANITY. Tell them that I say they all have one disability or another, but they are afraid to embrace it. Tell them that I say, if they do not know they have a disability in the morning, they will know they have it in the afternoon or in the evening so, they should embrace now. Tell them that I say, there is nothing negative or evil about you. The beginning of the disability journey (whether visible or invisible) is to accept your form of disability as part and parcel of who you are. Self-denial is very destructive, degrading and dehumanizing. You need to own your disability and be proud of yourself because that is part of your identity. It's not your fault that you look the way you do, but when you run and hide from who you are, whatever becomes of you would be your fault—your failures and your disappointments. Accept the person you are—your look and your limitations. Make peace with your disability because, for the rest of your life, you're going to be like that. Without acceptance, you will end up carrying all the baggage people have thrown on you. You will never value yourself but rather you will end up accepting what people think you are and what you cannot be. Without acceptance, you'll keep fighting against yourself and no one in history has ever won a battle they had to fight with their own being. You don't look how everybody else looks. Accept it. You can't do all the things everyone else is doing. Accept it. You can't be where everybody else can go. Accept it. But in the process of accepting who you are, ask yourself, *What can I do and do well? What are the skills I can learn within my limitations and excel at?* Once you identify these things, go for it and never stop.

There will be hurdles and barriers. Some of these barriers will be placed in your way by family, society, and the environment you find yourself in. And most importantly, most of these barriers will be placed in your way by your own self. Recognize the various barriers and develop the grit and determination to go around these barriers. It won't be easy. You'll fight against authorities and institutions to eschew these barriers. You'll have to be resolute, but fight fair and with respect. Some people in authority don't like to shift grounds but with respect, determination, and strength of character, you'll make way for yourself in the midst of all the opposition.

As a Christian, I learned I am a creation of God, and I am fearfully and wonderfully made in God's own image. I do not believe in the lies that the world tells me. I am not a cursed object! I am not a mistake! No, I am not an evil child. At least these are the things I know from my childhood that are true in my life. I hope you can identify your source of truth and live with it. The world is not just for people with disabilities so you need the truth to live your life.

And when you get to the point where your strength is known to you, resolve to project it all the way. Everything should be about your strength, and in this way, you can develop the confidence to feel at ease with yourself and the environment you find yourself in. If you play to your weakness, you'll give up very soon. Identify your strength, embrace it, work with it, and through that, you'll leave a mark in the minds of the people you work with and in the community you live in.

If you want to leave an indelible mark in your society, make a point to embark on some form of advocacy—it could be advocacy for yourself and others or action against unfavorable systems. Through advocacy work, you can bring about a lot of change to the society in which you live. Changes that previously people thought were unattainable. Everyone loves those who brought positive change into society and those who bring that change are not easily forgotten as long as others are enjoying the change they brought. Be a changemaker if you want your name written in the books of the society you live in. Try to leave a legacy behind for posterity to learn and practice from. Above all, try to celebrate the little victories that you achieve. Nobody will celebrate you, so find time for yourself, take a glass of water, and sip gently as you give yourself a pat on your shoulder to celebrate yourself in your own small way. If you have people around you who are your true friends or family members who share your vision and your dream, engage them to celebrate with you. Make it simple but very memorable because life is very short so seize the moment.

To the Policymaker

A lot of issues we face as people with disabilities come from policies or lack thereof. As a policy analyst myself, I see many policies thrown at our community that lack cultural responsiveness, empathy and human face. Some policies look good in some other jurisdictions. It doesn't mean it will work as well for our jurisdiction. Unfortunately, our leaders pick some of these policies, throw them at us, and expect them to deliver the aims for which they were made. Policies don't work that way. They have to be suited to the challenges we face in our cultural system in order for it to work. And this cultural lack of responsiveness mostly comes about due to the lack of engagement between policymakers and the real beneficiaries of the policies being drawn.

We need to engage all the stakeholders of the disability community to know their challenges firsthand if we want to draw up policies that would help make their problems bearable. There can be, "Nothing about us without us." We need people with disabilities around the discussion table. Policymakers can't cut people with disabilities off and assume they have extensive knowledge about the problems different people with disabilities go through. If the policy is about the blind, then, by all means, engage the blind. If the policies are for the physically disabled, then, by all means, engage the people who are physically disabled. We don't have to cram all disabilities into one pot and call it the same. No, they are not the same. That's why we draft policies that are beautiful and workable on paper but in the end, can't radiate the same beauty into the lives of those who need it. We engage the blind and assume the blind goes through the same challenges as the deaf.

For policies to work, policymakers need to bring the leaders of the various disability groups around the discussion table to discuss particular needs and solutions. They need to listen to us and have a heart of learning about our needs in order to find solutions to our needs. It won't take a day, I know, but it has to start from somewhere and it has to start now.

And lastly, policymakers need to back their policies with resources. We can have all the right policies but without the right tools to push the implementation of such policies, nothing will happen. This explains why most policies fail where they start. We can only change the world when we are armed with the right tools and resources. Policies themselves don't make a change. It's only when it's pushed with the right mindset, right people, and the right finances that change can be realized. It's time we stopped paying lip service to the issues of people with disabilities. It's time to make things work and I believe with the right culturally responsive policies, the right stakeholder engagements, and the right resources, things can change for the better and everyone involved will be proud for pushing the agenda of change.

To the Community and the Society as a Whole

Attitudinal change has been the central issue for all people with disabilities across the world. In African culture, especially in Ghanaian culture, it takes a village to raise a child and that is why it is important to engage and educate the community and the society to play a major part in the upbringing of any child with a disability. The community and society as a whole needs a paradigm shift and a very rapid attitudinal change towards people with disabilities in our communities. This is because the measure of norms or cultural beliefs that surround disability is very problematic. It is high time that we all take it upon ourselves to change the negative cultural belief systems in which our attitudes are so deeply rooted. Our attitudes towards a child with any form of disability, be it visible or invisible, are never embracing or welcoming in our culture.

I guess by this time, you will agree with me that DISABILITY IS PART OF HUMANITY. You will agree with me that, we should start talking about disability openly in our homes, schools (from kindergarten), market, farm, places of worship like churches, mosques, shrines, temples, alters, communities, affinity groups, etc., because it is part of us. You will also attest that disability binds us all whether you are black or white, poor or rich, young or old, you will or your somebody will have a disability one day before death strikes. This is why as a community, we need to start advocating for disability rights now so that in ten to twenty years' time, we will have a different generation with no stigma, no discrimination, and no plan of exclusion.

Our associated behaviors and beliefs towards our children with disabilities need to be positive. This is the only way that we can see something good in these children and promote them. The change in our attitudes will reflect on the agencies we establish from the school environment, health care, transportation, housing, insurance, and even their burial ceremonies.

Finally, this might sound too strong, but I realize I cannot write this book without sharing these special personal experiences of living abroad with you as a black woman from Africa. Indeed, the attitudes of the Western world towards disability are so different, very positive, but one thing we generally forget is that they also went through so many stages of stigma and marginalization which led them to fight for disability rights before they got to where they are today. Despite the fact that disability rights are fought and policies are in place, there are still some people who have prejudiced minds towards people with disabilities, especially people with disabilities from other cultures. Most people have robbed us of the truth about schooling and living abroad, especially we, the people with disabilities. Like many of you who have traveled outside your home countries, we have suffered a lot from external and internal forces. External forces can be the well-known demands or "attacks" from friends, family members, and even unknown friends for money, laptops, iPhones, etc. because you have traveled to the "land of the riches." That is not the focus of my conclusion because it is not any new thing to anybody who has traveled outside their home country. After all, we live a communal life, and we always bring goodies home even when we go to a funeral. I will also not dwell on the external forces so much because nobody will get it right since this is not the way America or the Western world is projected to us. Most of our predecessors who made this journey never told us about the realities on the ground, hence my intention to unveil some of the realities, especially for the child with a disability who is making this type of journey in the future. Of course, only a few people with disabilities made it this far and tried to document their experiences and share them with posterity. I deem it very necessary to unravel this knot because I was also in that oblivion for a long time. When I came to the U.S.A., I learned that we were deceived, that there are poor white people in the streets of America, and that money is never found on the street.

Yes, there is still mud and filth in America. It is not always glassy and full of roses as we see in the movies. The internal forces in this context imply the type of resistance we face in the land of the riches even if you have the energy to fight for your rights or advocate for yourself. The struggle for "acceptance" comes in different forms because it is inherent that the white man is superior and the black man is inferior, so you need to work extra hard to promote yourself. The goal to be recognized and "accepted" as part of them is a hard nut to crack. Despite all the knowledge you carry, the fight for your academic work to be valued and "accepted" as part of the intellectual discourse or property from the classroom to the community is debatable due to "lack of technical writing skills," which my friend Faith refers to as traces of Western or European schools of thought and colonial genealogy in the professoriate. Throughout the colonial lineage, there is always a preconceived assumption that you cannot perform better than the white man, and this challenges the black man to work extremely hard to prove himself as a perfectionist even if they are looking to be only average. In simple terms, there is a lot of racism in every sphere of life because it is systemic, even though you will find some whites who have recognized this cancer and are fighting with us. Let me tell you how racism showed up in my almost thirteen year's journey.

Racism has manifested itself in so many ways throughout my journey, but I can assure you that it calls for God's own divine power of identifying and connecting with changemakers in the community to fight with me. As you can see, I have been genuinely loved and supported by some committed white people but there were some who also made life very miserable for me at times. With my Christian values and beliefs, I know there is no racism in the kingdom of God because God created us all in His own image, but through all thirteen years of my experience in the USA school system, I can assure you that I have faced racism to the highest degree. I faced it in the classroom where my paper was deemed "useless" in a policy class because it was my own critical analysis of systemic issues, especially the cultural irresponsiveness of the educational policies thrown on us in Africa. In other words, my paper was an examination of systems, institutions, equipment, etc. that maintain able-centric thinking and over privilege the able-body. As you can see, it does not sound familiar and enticing because this seems to be connected to the critical analysis of the article "When Good Writing Means White Writing" by Marcos Gonsalez. Also, this whole process of incomprehensible writing skills keeps me thinking about a renowned scholar, Professor Elisio Macamo, and his speech about decolonization when I went to present another paper on ECAS 2017 in Geneva. He said, "Should you change the focus and call for the decolonization of the European mind? And when you follow suit on this call for the decolonization of minds, what kind of research program are you going to be standing up for? How are you going to vouch for its intellectual integrity without appearing contradictory? I mean, how do you rebel against something misrepresenting you when you know that your rebellion is intelligible to you and to others because you and those others know that your rebellion can only be articulated and rendered unintelligible within the framework laid down by the conceptual language which misrepresents and oppresses you?" Well, let me not take you to any deep critical analysis class but I would like to say, interestingly, that the same paper that was condemned as "useless" was published through the help of other professors who saw the good in me. Again, there are a lot of good white people and that is why you need to pray for God to connect you with the few who are there to make the change with you.

Another way racism and its power struggles have manifested in my life was when I was fully supported genuinely by four different faculty members from different departments to push my teaching assistantship work forward through a new curriculum building. Throughout my teaching evaluations, I have brought different perspectives about disability, including African perspectives, especially the Ghanaian perspectives, to the table of discussion hence their support to help me build a new syllabus to teach alongside with them.

They did their best to help me and a new syllabus was built but this dream was shattered by one single soul who had the power but did not see me to be part of the "elite" academia with them. Yes, that is the power dynamics in this journey because this individual was bold enough to tell me, "I will support you to complete your program, but not to get you a job." Wow. She was ready to help me finish my program but not to develop any part of me. Oh yes, she loves recommending me to people and using me as a resource person in any discussion around disability because I love sharing my personal story to empower the youth. All she could see me do in addition to my teaching and research assistantship job was helping to present in other classrooms, off-campus public speaking, and community outreaches. She would not endorse me or empower me to teach as other professors thought I could. To her, my extra support was classified as volunteerism but not a way into academia or a place among the "elite." Yes, this is the same person who thought she could write a page or two for my four-year dissertation to publish with me. This time, I was bold to say a big NO to her, and I will leave that to you, my reader, to digest or ponder over why I rejected such a "great" offer.

As you can see, even though she was so helpful in different ways, especially in writing good references and recommendations for whatever purposes, she could not see me, a black woman with a disability from Africa, with her in the same faculty meetings, teaching in the same classrooms, and advocating at the top for equal and equitable access to education for all minority groups. This is why I so much align my thoughts at times with Scott Woods in every single word he said when describing what racism is, as quoted below:

> "The problem is that white people see racism as conscious hate
> when racism is bigger than that. Racism is a complex system

of social and political levers and pulleys set up generations ago to continue working on the behalf of whites at other people's expense, whether whites know/like it or not. Racism is an insidious cultural disease. It is so insidious that it doesn't care if you are a white person who likes black people; it's still going to find a way to infect how you deal with people who don't look like you. Yes, racism looks like hate, but hate is just one manifestation. Privilege is another. Access is another. Ignorance is another. Apathy is another. And so on. So, while I agree with people who say no one is born racist, it remains a powerful system that we're immediately born into. It's like being born into air: you take it in as soon as you breathe. It's not a cold that you can get over. There is no anti-racist certification class. It's a set of socioeconomic traps and cultural values that are fired up every time we interact with the world. It is a thing you have to keep scooping out of the boat of your life to keep from drowning in it. I know it's hard work, but it's the price you pay for owning everything."

One important thing you should know is that I love volunteering. Volunteering is part of our African culture but we do not have a name for it. In view of this, we do not recognize it as a prerequisite requirement for any opened door because it is part of our community-building culture. We are always excited to help freely but I encourage you to start recording whatever you are volunteering for because it will help you in the future in any sphere of life, especially in job searches, and especially as a person with a disability.

I strongly believe that if we all change our attitudes and perceptions about disability, accept people with disabilities, and try to see what we need to help them develop, we will make a great productive community and society one day.

Again racism showed its ugly head when I reported the robbery of my room to the police and they told me they had more important issues, like assault, to deal with. I spent one month in Geneva with my Sista Mawutor. Upon my return from that presentation, I discovered that I was totally robbed including the couches, beds, clothes and even cooking utensils. The room was totally swept when I entered that evening. I thought I was in another room. I called my neighbor who was also new, and he knew nothing about it. I called my family back home and they were very optimistic in order to calm my nerves down because they reminded me that I am in the home of the brave and the land of the free. "You are in America. They will arrest the person soon by using their cameras or fingerprints so don't stress yourself." I took consolation in these words and slept on the ground that night.

The following day, I built some courage and called 911 (the police) about the robbery that occurred while I was outside the country to present a paper. They collected my details and came over for inspections. They realized that the thieves had brought a truck and packed our belongs through the back door in the bedroom. At this point, I was given a case number and connected to Officer John, so I was sure that they would find my things for me. After three weeks, I heard nothing, so my friends encouraged me follow up. When I called, Officer John was connected to me on the phone and he was very simple:

> Officer John: Mum, when exactly did you say your things were stolen?

> Me: Please, I cannot tell because I was not in the country for a whole month.

> Officer John: Well, we need the exact date and time to move forward.

> Me: Please, could you check the cameras around here to see if you can find anything?

> Officer John: Your building does not have any cameras so there is no way we can trace your lost items. I think we will get back to you next week if we do not have any evidence from you.

> Me: Just like that?

> Officer John: Yes, because we have more important caseloads like assaults so we might close your case in a month.

Indeed, in exactly one month I was called and told that they had closed my case. That was how my hopes were shuttered and the American cameras and fingerprints could not work for me as projected in the movies. Later, some of my American friends told me that this is pure racism because this would never happen to them.

The fact is, no African can believe thieves cannot be traced in America despite all the forensic science and psychology today. This is unbelievable, but it did happen to me. I leave that to your discretion because we are all entitled to our opinions.

CHAPTER 16 QUESTIONS:

–From your perspective, how does race affect disability?

–From intersectional social justice lens, what would you do as a change agent to break down systemic barriers people with disabilities and other identities go through daily?

–How do you help people who deal with issues of exclusion and marginalization?

–Finally, do you think you are a part of the solution or a part of the problem? In your own special way, how will you build an inclusive, diverse, and just community?

Epilogue

Finally, as you can see, we have come to the end of the first part of my journey. I poured out myself to you and you know almost everything about my past, my present and hints of my future. You can see I went through hell in life, but the good Lord has been so gracious with me. I lost my own daughter, lost my Mum yet, I am not dead. I am still here recounting my story to you to see the life of a person with a disability through my lens so that you can make some positive decisions. I believe some questions have emerged for you because of self-scrutiny, self–reflection, or self-actualization with regards to disability and pursuit of equitable opportunities.

In this book, we have questions below every chapter and those questions prompt us to think critically about the existing negative belief systems, cultural practices, concepts, frameworks, and approaches surrounding disability. You might be thinking about how this can be re–conceptualized to foster greater inclusivity, equal opportunities, and equitable access. At this juncture, I am sure you were able to answer all the questions for yourself to change the negative narratives in your own small way. If nothing has changed in you yet, you can still try to find answers to the following brainstorming questions as we wrap up the book.

Keep thinking about:

a) What is your own definition of disability now?

b) What questions have emerged for you as a result of reading this book and why?

c) How do you think we can re-conceptualize disability for equitable opportunities?

d) How can societal negative attitudes and perceptions towards disability be transformed to promote inclusivity and to eliminate discrimination?

e) What are the key barriers or stereotypes that prevent individuals with disabilities from accessing education, healthcare, accessible housing, employment, transportation etc.?

f) What policy frameworks and legal protections are necessary to ensure the rights and independent living of people with disabilities?

g) What is your definition of diversity, equity, and inclusion in an ableist world?

h) What is one embarrassing mistake you hope never to make with a person of another race?

i) What one simple change would you like to make after reading this book?

j) What do you think should be the next book title?

Moving forward this may seem repetitive, but I really want it to sink in your heart and soul. I would like to challenge you to embrace disability as part of humanity and not as something negative.

Again, let it sink in that disability is part of humanity, and everybody has some strength and some weakness. It is not because of our disability that we are not able to do certain things. We are as strong and as weak as anyone reading this book. The truth is, everyone has a disability, but no one wants to embrace it because of the stigma around it. This is why you and I need to decide and make the choice of changing this systemic and destructive narrative. Imagine how the world would have been if you had been educated from kindergarten about disabilities that everyone has, just like how we all have to eat to survive. Some people have it either in the morning, afternoon, or evening? That is, you might have it from the womb or after birth. This is why you need to learn about it at home from your parents before you learn about it at school, and in the community to normalize it. The fact is there is nothing wrong with us, but society is always disabling us therefore everyone needs to learn the truth about disability.

Recently, in the process of overhauling the system and building transformational leaders and change agents, I have started a movement in academia through my new Global Disability Studies Course at the University of Vermont-USA. It is an online asynchronous course so that everyone can take it and make the changes wherever they find themselves around the globe. It is also open to all categories of students from undergraduates, graduates, professionals, and non-traditional students. This online asynchronous course won me the prestigious 2022 Prelock Online Asynchronous Award which went viral. Why am I telling you all this? This is to encourage you to be change oriented to start something in your own small way to change the negative narratives about disability. You might not have access to students, but you have your co-workers, family members, team workers, youth groups or grannies' association. Who said you cannot make the change you want in your own small way? It is all about determination, perseverance, resilience, and selflessness in an ableist world. My main goals are to dismantle systemic barriers, to build and empower people globally, to understand the realities of disability so that they can build advocacy campaigns in their chosen communities. I strongly believe we can all change greater minds from homes, the classroom, and the community since change starts from these places.

Watch out for my next book to hear more about how the Global Disability Studies Course is expanding across the USA, Africa, Asia, Europe, etc.

Acknowledgements

I acknowledge that I have been supported by a lot of people in my life and I cannot thank them enough. I have an unending list of my helpers (some are dead), so I say God bless you for the role you played in my life. I acknowledge all my black, brown, and white folks who have seen the good in me and pull it out to be in this book. *Akpe nami kakaka.*

A big thank you to my sincere editors: Nesta Jojoe Erskine, Chris Worla Essikpe, Kim Brittenham, and Godfread Ofori who read through and gave me harsh but constructive feedback. Mama, Kim, thank you very much for all your time and wisdom you put into shaping this book.

Biography

Sefakor's personal experience as a woman of color with a physical disability has shaped her journey as an international advocate for underrepresented especially, people with disabilities from around the globe. Her experiences include serving as an international disability rights advocate, educator, researcher, and policy analyst for the UN Convention on the Rights of Persons with Disability (UNCRPD), and as the Resource Center Coordinator of the Ghana Education Service. She has been a staunch supporter of inclusive education for people with disabilities and lobbied successfully with other advocates in Ghana for the establishment of the Disability Law (Act 715) of Ghana as well as the ratification of the UNCRPD. She has won so many international awards including the International Service Award from the Association of University Centers on Disabilities (AUCD), Ford Foundation International Fellowship award and the International Alliance of Women (TIAW) award. Sefakor is the Founder of Enlightening and Empowering People with Disabilities in Africa (EEPD AFRICA). She presented on so many platforms including the American Educational Research Association AERA (SIG RWE), New England Educational Organization (NEERO), African Studies Association (ASA) and European Conference on African Studies – Switzerland (ECAS). Her work represented an attempt to transform her experiences into a coherent intellectual critique, and, in the process, to make sense of the shortcomings and idiosyncrasies that underlie contemporary responses to human rights abuses in schools. In

2016, Sefakor was named the 6th most influential disabled person in the world. Sefakor also teaches the Global Disability Studies course and Race and Racism Course as adjunct at the University of Vermont. At Saint Michael's College, she teaches Disability Justice and Ethical Leadership and Disability Policies. She won the prestigious Prelock 2022 award for her excellent asynchronous online course at the University of Vermont. Sefakor works with Vermont Center for Independent Living with all students across the State of Vermont between the ages of 14 to 26 to build their self-advocacy skills and strategies. She serves on so many boards including the World Learning Global Advisory Council, The High-Level Political Forum of UN (HLPF), African Association of Disability and Self-Advocacy (AADISAO), The Free Wheelchair Mission, The Presidents Commission on Inclusive Excellence (PCIE) of UVM, and the ADA Taskforce of UVM. Sefakor co-authored the books "Disability in the Global South: The Critical Handbook", "Next Generation Digital Tools and Application for Teaching and Learning Enhancement 1ST Edition" and the "Handbook of Research on Contemporary Issues in Multicultural and Global Education.